LETTERS TO MY DEPARTED SON

LETTERS TO MY DEPARTED SON

Dear Brandon

Constance Spight

ARCHWAY PUBLISHING

Archway Publishing books may be ordered through booksellers or by contacting:

Archway Publishing
1663 Liberty Drive
Bloomington, IN 47403
www.archwaypublishing.com
844-669-3957

Photo cover - Image1 - Painted by D. Green
Back Exterior cover - Image33 - Jim Waye/Photographer, J. Arlington Photography

All Scripture quotations are taken from The Holy Bible, New International Version®, NIV® Copyright © 1973, 1978, 1984, 2011 by Biblica, Inc.® Used by permission. All rights reserved worldwide.

ISBN: 978-1-6657-1578-2 (sc)
ISBN: 978-1-6657-1577-5 (hc)
ISBN: 978-1-6657-1579-9 (e)

Library of Congress Control Number: 2021924040

Print information available on the last page.

Archway Publishing rev. date: 01/31/2022

*In memory of my son, Brandon Lee Spight
whose incredible existence gave me life.*

Constance Jackson Spight

CONTENTS

PREFACE

Astronomical odds seemed to define your brief, bright life, Brandon. We thought of you as our one-in-a-million child, a gift from God. At times your dad and I didn't believe we would conceive a child.

Yet when you were born you looked absolutely perfect. And you were! After giving birth, even though I was heavily sedated, I asked your dad if you had all your fingers and toes. You had ten fingers, ten toes, huge brown eyes, and a heart-melting smile.

How could we possibly have dreamed there was a small imperfection deep within your head that ultimately would force you to make a life-or-death decision while you were still in your teens? And we certainly had no reason to expect that you would leave us so soon, just ten days before your eighteenth birthday.

Ultimately, Brandon, you chose the young, vibrant life you knew over the grim uncertainty that might have been. You were wise far beyond your birthdays and accomplished more in your short stay with us than some people do over decades. You were a natural, sensational golfer and a dedicated student at University of Detroit Jesuit High School and Academy. You were a charismatic leader, an inspiring tutor, budding philosopher, devoted friend, and loving son. Very simply put, you were a great kid.

Though your time with us was far too fleeting and we miss you dearly every single day, we are proud of the son we created and appreciative of our life together. Your life and legacy exemplify the power of the human spirit and the capacity to instinctively connect with others of any age, ultimately resulting in the positive impact you had on numerous other lives. It's as if that were your mission, your purpose for being on earth. Our request for letters written to you posthumously, some of which are included in this book, *Dear Brandon*, was answered by more than a hundred responses from classmates, relatives, friends, teachers, and others who knew and loved you well. You were on a mission. It is now our mission to continue what you started. This book is our "Plan B."

The proceeds from this book will be designated to the Brandon Lee Spight Memorial Foundation (BLSMF), a nonprofit organization that has provided scholarships since 2007 to young men attending University of Detroit Jesuit High School and Academy. We have partially endowed the fund to honor your memory and celebrate your legacy at the school that meant so much to you. As of late 2020, we have raised more than $50,000. We have 20 percent of our goal of $250,000.

The letters and memories to you are an essential component of *Dear Brandon*. However, Bran, as your parents, we felt it was important to share the depth and details of your life through our own recollections as well. It was an extraordinary life, a life that nearly didn't happen.

1

"WE'VE NOTICED A SMALL BLEED ..."

Dear Brandon,

The telephone call—and thus your diagnosis and the beginning of the catastrophic events that would change our family forever—came after school on January 17, 2007. You were lying on the family room couch, Bran, seeking to soothe yet another headache. Haley, our cat since she was six weeks old, was nestled close to your chest in what seemed to be an attempt to heal you, as if she knew you weren't well.

You'd been complaining about frequent headaches—searing, withering, and debilitating—since shortly after New Year's Day. The headaches had sapped your everyday vitality and made getting through your senior-year classes and semester exams at University of Detroit Jesuit High School a struggle.

Your dad and I first thought it might be just a case of the flu. An especially nasty strain, Influenza A (H3), was going around that year, and you exhibited some of the symptoms, such as severe headaches and vomiting. When our primary care doctor, David Wolf, examined you, he asked you to perform a series of simple movements, which included standing up quickly and tilting your head side to side. He had no diagnosis or prescription, although I later learned he suspected meningitis. He referred us to a neurologist, who had you perform similar movements and then said, "I think we need to order an MRI." Based upon my past experiences, a magnetic resonance imaging (MRI) provides detailed images of organs and tissues in the body. Neither one of us had any initial concerns regarding the test. I think we both just wanted answers. The MRI was administered on January 16, 2007.

Now it's January 17, a day after the MRI, when the neurologist called with the results. "Mrs. Spight, we've noticed a small bleed within Brandon's brain."

The neurologist continued talking, but my mind had fled the unwanted conversation and retreated into a corner to avoid his words. *A small bleed?* I thought. *What is he talking about?* I walked down the first-floor hallway to the front of the house, Bran, because I didn't want you to hear me.

With my brain still attempting to comprehend the doctor's words, I consciously returned to the phone conversation and said, "I'm sorry. What did you say?"

The neurologist was extremely patient with me. He repeated, "We've noticed a small bleed. It's about two centimeters in size. We really don't think it's ..."

And my brain started to retreat again. *He's not talking about my son,* my inner voice kept saying over and over. *This cannot be real. There must be a mistake.*

"I'm sorry," I said to the doctor. "You're going to think I'm crazy, but I'm really not understanding. Could you start over, please?"

In all, the neurologist had to repeat himself three times because every ounce of me was fighting against accepting the reality of his words. I heard him say that we needed to take you to yet another specialist, a vascular neurologist. I struggled to remain focused, but I did hear him say he didn't think the bleed was serious. Oh, if only! If only he had been right.

You didn't hear any of this, Bran. By the time I hung up with the neurologist, I had gone upstairs into the office/study room. I was falling apart. I could feel warmth around my neck and my eyes beginning to swell with tears. I was not ready for you to see me in that state of despair, especially since your dad wasn't home.

I sat quietly for a few seconds. I couldn't call your dad, Bran, because I felt I needed to tell him face-to-face. I called Lisa Stout, our family's self-taught, go-to person for dealing with medical issues.

In a calm, reassuring voice, she said, "Okay. Let's get on the computer and try to find a vascular neurologist."

We got on our respective computers, still on our telephones, and began searching. I was determined to find a vascular neurologist. Suddenly it occurred to me: *Oh my God, why are we searching? I need to call Dr. Wolf!*

I told Lisa I'd call her back, got Dr. Wolf on the phone, and explained the situation. He gave me the name and number of a doctor to contact. He said, "He is one of the best vascular neurologists in the area. Tell them I referred you." Ominously he added, "Tell them you need to get in to see him as soon as possible."

I immediately called the doctor's office, known to be a respected expert in the treatment of cerebrovascular diseases. The receptionist said the soonest she could work in Brandon was two weeks away, on January 31.

"That's the earliest appointment you have, you're sure?" I asked, trying to mask the panic in my voice.

She assured me it was, so I made the appointment. Then I called Dr. Wolf back.

"Oh no no," he said. "That's not soon enough. Let me call the doctor's office."

Within minutes, the receptionist called me back. The doctor could see us earlier, January 24. I was appreciative but still felt it was a long seven days out.

She said something about our insurance not covering the office visit. "You'll have to pay for the visit when you arrive. It will be $450. We require payment when you come in."

"Fine!" I exclaimed.

Really, I thought, *I don't care how much it cost! This is my son, my heart!*

Shortly after confirming the appointment, your dad, came home. I took him upstairs to our bedroom, out of earshot, before he could even say hello to you, Bran.

When I told your dad, his face froze for what seemed like an eternity. He looked at me and then looked away, saying nothing. Finally he asked, "Have you told Brandon?"

"No, not yet."

As we slowly walked downstairs, I knew I would have to provide the narrative and I had to appear strong even though my pounding head and tightening stomach indicated my strength was waning. We approached you, half-asleep on the sofa.

"We need to speak to you," I said, sitting down next to you.

Virgil sat across from you, and I explained what the neurologist had said. I could tell you were concentrating and focused on absorbing my every word. Even as a seventeen-year-old, you had an astute ability to digest and dissect complicated issues.

You thought for a long moment. "So my brain is bleeding?"

"No, no, Brandon," I said. "You just have a small area where a vessel is—"

"Mom," you stopped me. "My brain is bleeding."

"No. There is an area ... a blood vessel in your brain that is bleeding, Brandon. But we don't know how serious this is right now. We're going to see the doctor next week." Hearing myself say "next week" seemed again totally inadequate.

You just sat there. I attempted to downplay the urgency of the situation. I didn't want to scare you, but I think you knew I was scared. You had a way of seeing deep within my soul.

This day would forever remain etched in my memory even if it held no other significance, but January 17 is a day of celebration for our family because it's your dad's birthday.

"Brandon," I said, "it's your dad's birthday. And we're going to keep our plans and go out for dinner."

I figured the best way to deal with the frightening unknown was to continue to carry out a familiar family ritual. You know it's our family tradition to celebrate every birthday with a special restaurant dinner.

You looked up at me. "Mom, I am not hungry. I really don't feel like going."

I didn't want to go either. I just thought we could make an attempt at normalcy and try to forget, even momentarily, about this distressing news. I wanted to acknowledge your dad's birthday, but I wasn't sure how to convince you. I also was not leaving you at home. That was out of the question. You turned to look at your dad, who was staring straight at you, not saying a word. That unspoken connection was all it took.

"Okay," you said, "I'll go."

So we went out to dinner, as we always did on your dad's birthday. We had made reservations at Ruth's Chris Steak House, one of Dad's favorites. You liked it too because you followed in your father's carnivorous footsteps. You both were big steak eaters.

But not on this night though. This night was so very different. I tried to make small talk during dinner, but it was breath wasted. You and your dad were the jokesters who usually initiated mealtime laughter. But Dad didn't feel like talking, and you just didn't feel well at all. My heart broke and my fear mounted as I sat watching you move your food around on the plate, taking only a few bites. We asked to have your meal wrapped up and took it home with us.

Over the next week, we kept to the usual routine. But I know we all felt on edge. You started the second semester of your senior year. The headaches were ever-present, but you fought through the pain and attempted to focus on finishing up college applications due soon.

One night, your godsisters, Kezia McAllister and Erica

Alexander (Lisa's daughters), visited. Kezia helped you finish the college applications, while Erica made taco soup, one of your favorites. That evening, the college applications were complete and ready for the mail, but you only had an appetite for a spoonful or two of your favorite soup.

Finally January 24 came, the day to see the specialist. That's when we learned the astronomical odds against anyone, much less our child, developing this small bleed.

The doctor explained three possible scenarios were causing the bleeding in your brain. It could be a tumor or a cavernous angioma, a collection of malformed blood vessels in the shape of caverns. The third possibility was a blood vessel disorder known as an arteriovenous malformation (AVM), a far more perilous diagnosis. An AVM is a congenital abnormality in which blood vessels literally are entangled during the development of the fetus. This can develop in various locations in the body.

At that time, the doctor did not believe it was an AVM because you were functioning relatively well, still performing in school, and active with your friends. A bleeding AVM, he said, would make it difficult for you to do everyday activities. Brandon, I believe you asked how common this condition was. He told us that only 3 percent of the population has AVMs and most live their entire lives without incident. Of the 3 percent who have the condition, he said, only 2–3 percent of those people ever develop bleeding. Both you and I were simply flabbergasted by those figures. You literally were one in a million, in a way we never could have anticipated or desired.

But we didn't know that yet for sure. The doctor stressed that he thought you had a cavernous angioma, Bran, and that actually reassured us. A cavernous angioma often heals itself, and he expected your body would heal by absorbing the bleeding over the next few weeks.

But he also laid out the worst-case scenario, what the

consequences would be if the diagnosis were a bleeding AVM. The bleed was deeply embedded in the rear right side of your brain, he said. If it were an AVM, that presented dire problems.

He further explained that surgery might be needed to repair an AVM. If surgery were performed, which couldn't happen until the bleeding stopped and the blood was absorbed into your body, chances are you would end up with a deficit.

I asked, "What kind of deficit?"

He responded, "Paralysis. Brain damage."

As the doctor began to explain different surgical procedures, you stood up from the exam room table. You would hear none of it. "No surgery!" you said. You were very assured and straightforward.

I sat there shocked, stunned by your words. You knew I would try to talk you out of this decision. You looked at me with those large, beautiful brown eyes and repeated it. "Mom, no surgery." You were adamant. I was speechless.

I thought, *He's only seventeen. How can he say that with such certainty?* But this is you, Brandon. You were confident to a fault. As much as your decision was troublesome, I convinced myself that it was a possibility we would not face.

At any rate, it was a certainty that I didn't want to question then. In the weeks ahead, this moment and the conviction of your response shaped our ultimate decision, which still haunts me. But on that particular day in the doctor's office, he stressed that an AVM was not the likely diagnosis.

I had prepared a list of questions that the doctor patiently answered. He said that Brandon could still go to school and participate in everyday activities. I think we both left his office feeling reassured and hopeful that what you had was only a cavernous angioma and that the blood would be absorbed into your body.

"He must be good, Mom," you commented as you pointed out his degrees and awards displayed on the office walls.

We were in watch-and-wait mode. You continued to function as best you could. The recommended medication you took for your headache pain was Tylenol.

You went back to school the next day, Bran. I held your arm as we walked up the stairs into school. Another mom noticed and stopped to ask me if everything were all right. I didn't have it in me to give details. "We hope it is," I responded.

But soon you stopped sleeping in your own room on the third floor of our home. We have an older house with older windows, and it gets cold up there in the winter. You moved into the guest room on the second floor, down the hall from our bedroom.

"I'm going to sleep down here," you declared.

I'm not sure your move was due to the drafty windows or the need to be closer to your parents. The latter came to fruition when your headache pain was so unbearable that you sometimes slept in the bed with your dad and me while I held you as if you were a toddler again.

Just a few days later, you were taking a bath when I heard a loud noise coming from the bathroom. Now at seventeen, you were not about to let me see you naked anymore! So I called out for your dad to come help. I thought you must have slipped in the tub, and I was thinking, *Oh my God, did he hit his head?*

You shouted out, "Mom, I'm fine! I'm fine." You kept repeating it, most likely for my peace of mind, but I had your dad go in to check on you anyway to make sure.

A few days later at dinner, you forced yourself to eat a little bit of food. But you couldn't keep it down and threw up on your plate.

"Mom, I'm really not hungry." You sighed. "I just want to lay down."

You went upstairs to sit in one of the recliners in our bedroom to watch TV. I soon joined you in the other recliner. I must have drifted off because the sound of a loud thud in the hallway jolted me awake. I ran out to the hall and found that you had toppled over and crashed into the wall.

"I got up to use the bathroom," you said. Your voice sounded okay, but your body seemed contorted. You didn't say anything else.

The look on your face was one I had seen before on the face of my mother, your granny. The dazed, faraway look in your eyes and your inability to move, I knew you were having a stroke, Bran. I could hear a voice screaming for your dad. It was mine!

Your dad and I frantically got you dressed and helped you out to the car. Your dad did not want to delay one second in getting you to the hospital. I kept talking to you in the car. I told you to open your eyes, and you did. I told you to move your hand, and you lifted your right hand and gave a halfhearted wave. But I could see that the left side of your body did not move.

This was Tuesday, January 30, thirteen days after your diagnosis. You were admitted to William Beaumont Hospital in Royal Oak, Michigan.

2

OUR LITTLE MIRACLE

During certain portions of my life, I was often known as someone other than Connie. This is not meant as a complaint, just an admission that my identity was often attached to someone else's. As a child, I was known as Charles and Quincy's baby girl. Then as an adolescent and teen, I was known as your Uncle Clyde's little sister, which was not surprising since we were close in age and attended the same high school. I was called Constance—or, more often, "ma'am"—when I served as a commander in the Detroit Police Department. Later after I married, I was best known as Virgil's wife. But Mom, Brandon's mom, or Little Tiger's mom were my favorite titles of all. That's because of you, Brandon Lee Spight, our beautiful, artistic, precocious, gifted son.

And while I'm retired now from an exciting, fulfilling, and often challenging career, my job always ran a distant second to the all-important job of being your mom. You were my most worthy accomplishment. Whatever else I do in my life will not surpass giving birth to and raising you.

How I would feel being a mom was not evident to me for many years because having children, although a dream of mine, was not always in my plans. My parents did not go to college, but they were acutely aware of the importance of a college education. And they knew they wanted me, the youngest of their three children and their only daughter, to attend college.

I am a product of the Detroit Public Schools system. In fact, in an almost unbelievable combination of irony and foreshadowing, that's where I first encountered your dad, but not as a classmate. Your dad, who is eleven years older than I am, was the in-house police officer at Mumford High School when I was a student there.

The running joke among our friends was that Virgil must have robbed the cradle by dating me when I was a student at Mumford High School, but I actually did not know him back then. Truthfully I did not want to!

All the high school kids were afraid of Virgil because he really kept everybody in line. I never got into any trouble, so I didn't have any dealings with him at all. All I remember is the image of this big, bad, tough-looking police officer walking around the school with his hat pulled way down over his eyes and never a smile on his face. We all ran the other way when we saw him coming!

I was a good student at Mumford, which earned me an acceptance to Michigan State University. So off I went to East Lansing in the fall of 1970, not really knowing which career to pursue. The other thing I didn't know—and didn't find out until sometime after I graduated—was that my father, a Chrysler crane operator, had informed my two brothers, your Uncles Carl and Clyde, that he could afford to send only one of his children to college. And it was going to be me! How much more pressure would I have felt to set stronger career goals had I known that when I was in school! But as I said, your grandfather's decision was kept a complete secret from me.

I honestly don't think your Uncle Clyde cared because he hadn't expressed an interest in college. But I think your Uncle Carl wanted to go to college, and I thought, *Oh God, he must hate me!*

As you know, I majored in criminal justice, a field I have specifically told you to avoid! Today, Brandon, when I hear kids say they're going to major in criminal justice, I ask them a ton of questions. Based on my experience, I don't think criminal justice is a wise degree for someone to obtain unless they have a firm idea of how they intend to use it or if they plan to pursue an advanced degree. So when you announced you would obtain your degree in political science and later attend law school, I was elated, especially since as a youngster, much to my dismay, you expressed a desire to be a police officer.

My plan was to work as a probation or parole officer, but when I graduated in 1974, those positions were scarce. However, the Detroit Police Department was hiring, so I applied, thinking I'd be assigned to the Women's Division, which investigated abuse and neglect complaints specific to women and children. To my great surprise, I hired in just when the Women's Division was being disbanded in 1975 and female and male officers were assigned to street patrol in the same squad cars for the first time in Detroit's history. Believe me when I tell you, the male officers did not want to be working with women!

It was a challenging time, Bran, to put it very mildly. Your grandmother was one of many people who did not like the idea at all, but I assured her that I had a long-range strategy. I planned to work for Detroit Police for five years and then join the Federal Bureau of Investigation (FBI). But instead, lo and behold, I ended up staying with the Detroit Police Department for twenty-five years.

Your granny was disappointed and concerned that my first precinct assignment was to patrol Detroit's east side at the 15th Precinct. I grew up on the northwest side and rarely went to the east side of town. My patrol route was along streets and in neighborhoods I'd never heard of. I was being launched out of my comfort zone and forced to learn how to navigate new territory.

"Don't they know where you live?" my mother huffed.

"Ma, they don't care where I live!"

It was bad enough that the male officers didn't want women

partnering with them. It also didn't help that most of the time I had no idea where I was or how to get to the locations dispatched via Scout Car radio. Remember, this was during the time before MapQuest, GPS equipment, and smartphones. I was forced to become familiar with the new surroundings, landmarks, and neighborhoods, a critical part of my job. My veteran male partners often let me fumble along, without offering to help with directions or even gesturing to turn right or left.

I remember one rookie shift in particular. I was paired with a veteran male officer, and as I drove the patrol route, he didn't utter a word until, that is, I had steered the car out of the city limits.

At shift's end, my lieutenant said to me, "Jackson (my maiden name), how did it go?"

I told him my partner displayed an obvious contempt for female officers and that I was legitimately concerned for my safety. I never was assigned to work with him again.

Later in my career when I was promoted to sergeant, the men in my command sought to test me. I was a new sergeant in 1983 and assigned to the 10th Precinct on the west side near Livernois Avenue and Elmhurst Street.

On my first day on the precinct desk, an officer accompanied me to check the precinct's cell block. I didn't say a word, nor did he, as we walked by a cell with a dummy hanging from the ceiling. The guys expected me to freak out, but I didn't break stride.

"You can take the dummy down now," I told them as I returned to the front desk that was surrounded by officers, obviously disappointed that I had remained calm.

Your dad told me I should have written them up, but I thought my controlled demeanor made for a better impression.

Speaking of your dad, I became acquainted with him anew in 1975 while I was attending the police academy. Our paths crossed while he was attending Officer's Candidate School after being promoted to the rank of lieutenant.

"You went to Mumford, didn't you? Don't you remember me?" he asked.

I certainly did not.

"You've got to remember me. I'm Spight," he exclaimed. "I was the Mumford police officer." He knew every face in the building back then, he said, and mine hadn't changed in the years since.

"Oh, you're Spike," I said. That's what we called him back then, not knowing the correct name was "Spight." And "Spike," without question, fit the demeanor he displayed in the Mumford High halls.

I was seven years on the force before I encountered your dad again. We were both assigned to 1300 Beaubien, police headquarters downtown. One day, he asked me to go to lunch with him. I didn't think it was a date. It was my thirtieth birthday, so I just thought he was being a nice guy.

Our first official date was to a Temptations concert. I would later come to learn—and you too—that your dad loved the Temptations. I know you remember that as a kid growing up, you attended every performance with us. And guess what, Bran? We still go to every performance.

I was still a police officer when your dad and I started seeing each other, but your dad had already made lieutenant. After a while, he became my confidant. He was a tremendous help and support to me as I began earning promotions and moving up the ranks in the department, aiding me with insights based upon his experience.

My duties expanded to include learning about computers and information technology, and I was one of the first black female officers to work in the Information Systems Section (ISS) for the Detroit Police Department. When I was later promoted to sergeant, to my surprise, I continued my assignment at the ISS. Your dad guided me through that transition because it can be problematic returning to the same command and suddenly having authority over your coworkers.

He kept reminding me, "You're a sergeant now; you're a supervisor." He helped me in similar fashion with every promotion I received.

But when we first started dating, we barely talked about work. I discovered there was another side to his cool, ultra-confident, almost-cocky work persona. I was surprised to learn that tough cop "Spike" was a country boy at heart, born in Mississippi. Your dad always loved to be outdoors, and fishing was his passion.

Your dad was hesitant to date me. He said he'd never dated a cop before, and to this day, no evidence to the contrary has surfaced. On April 20, 1985, three years after our first date, we were married. It was my first marriage, but your dad's second. I feared marriage, Bran, I think, because both my brothers' marriages had ended in divorce and I feared a similar outcome. So I avoided marriage.

As a little girl, I had dreamed of getting married and having children, but I eventually convinced myself that it was just a silly idea ingrained into little girls' heads. When marriage finally happened, much later for me than for my friends, I told myself I probably would never have children. After you were born though, I couldn't imagine life without you.

As you know, your father has four other children, and I think he often regrets not spending enough time with them when they were younger, but his obsession with building his career took precedence. You see, your dad came through the Detroit Police Department at a time of great challenge when the civil rights struggle was forcing necessary upheaval in the police force, the city of Detroit, and the entire country. Determined to correct his past mistakes, your dad referred to you as his "second chance." Suffice it to say, you never lacked attention or time with your dad.

As your dad told you many times, "I was going to school, and working whenever they told me to work. And I was working hard because I wanted to be something in the police department. And I ended up doing pretty good. I joined the force in 1964, and when

I made sergeant in 1972, some officers told me, 'You can't make sergeant! No black man has ever made sergeant that fast here!' But I made it. And I told them I was going to make lieutenant too. When I was in the air force, it was exactly the same situation. Too many times, I was told what I couldn't accomplish. And in 1975, I made lieutenant with DPD while also attending the University of Detroit in the evenings."

You've heard these stories, Brandon, about how your dad rose through the ranks because of his work ethic, talent, and grit. In 1993, he was promoted to inspector. Later that year, I was too. In 1995, then-Police Chief Isaiah "Ike" McKinnon called me into his office to tell me that some promotions to commander were upcoming. The chief said he wanted to promote me, in part, because the department needed more women in that role. I asked if your dad were slated to become a commander too. The chief asked if that would be a problem.

"It's not going to be a problem for Virgil if I'm promoted to commander, but it's going to be a problem for me," I told the chief, particularly if it meant that Virgil wasn't going to get a promotion he so richly deserved.

The chief assured me that Virgil was slated for a promotion later that year. A few months after I became commander, your dad got a promotion too.

At one point while your dad was commander of the 2nd Precinct, I was assigned as commander to the adjoining 8th Precinct. The two precincts shared a boundary, Grand River Avenue. This prompted some lighthearted ribbing. Once during a Board of Police commissioners meeting, I quipped, "As a matter of fact, Chief McKinnon, I believe Grand River Avenue should be renamed Spight Boulevard."

Your dad wanted to have a family with me; he wanted to have only one child. This made complete sense to me as I felt that raising one child really was sufficient in this day and age, given the astronomical costs involved in raising and educating kids. So I told your dad, "Okay, no problem."

After our decision, we tried to get pregnant, but it just wasn't happening. A checkup by my gynecologist revealed large fibroids in my uterus. Now that wasn't an unusual diagnosis in and of itself. Such benign tumors appear in up to 30 percent of all women, and African-American women are more prone to them and tend to develop them at a younger age. However, in my case, the fibroids were so large that they were preventing conception. And if I did become pregnant, the doctor warned that I most likely would miscarry because of the growths. I sought second and third opinions, which confirmed the initial diagnosis.

After prayer, contemplation, and many discussions with your dad, I decided to undergo surgery to remove the fibroids. A myomectomy is the medical term. My doctor explained the possible surgical complications, which included hemorrhage, anemia, and uterine rupture in subsequent pregnancies, to name a few. I so greatly wanted a child that I was willing to take the risk. I wanted Virgil and me to have a child of our own. I wanted you.

The surgery to remove the fibroids did not go smoothly or well. While in recovery, I developed serious internal bleeding and nearly bled to death. Your dad and your Uncle Clyde said I literally turned white in post-op. I received several blood transfusions in rapid succession, and my doctor warned that if they couldn't stop the bleeding quickly, they would have no choice but to perform a hysterectomy.

Fortunately my doctor was able to perform an intervention and blood-therapy treatment that were sufficient to stop the internal bleeding. However, I then developed a bowel obstruction that required yet another form of treatment. I ended up staying in the hospital for thirty days. Your dad often says that those were the most frightening days he had ever experienced. We had only been married for two years, and already he was faced with the possibility of losing me.

I was incredibly fortunate that a hysterectomy was not necessary, but the entire ordeal had sufficiently spooked everyone. While I remained in the hospital recovering, your granny, with a look of supportive concern, whispered to me, "Honey, you know, maybe it's just not meant for you to have a baby. You can't let yourself worry about it."

Even then though, I was thinking, *They didn't have to give me a hysterectomy, so maybe it is meant to be.*

Perhaps another doctor would have made the alternative decision to perform a hysterectomy. But my doctor had heard my words and respected my wishes while maintaining my health as a priority. No way could all of this be luck or a series of random coincidences. We could see the hand of God working in our lives.

Bran, as I recall discussing my hospital ordeal with you, I also showed you my left hand and explained how fortune-telling palm readers look at the various lines in your hand to forecast your fate. I continued by pointing out what I believed to be my lifeline, the crease on my palm that curves down from between my thumb and my forefinger toward my wrist. I showed you how mine has a noticeable break, almost like a fork in the road, and then it extends all the way down to my wrist. I believe those horrible days in the hospital, when I could have lived or died, were my fork in the road.

After which, you of course looked at your own hand and exclaimed, "Mom, look! My line is short, and you can barely see it!"

At those words, I was momentarily speechless and felt distressingly irresponsible for engaging in this topic with you that I knew very little about. Had I ever looked at your hand before?

I responded, "Oh, Brandon, this is just based on a palm-reading practice with hundreds of interpretations. There is no scientific proof."

I swiftly returned to the hospital story. Now that the fibroids were gone, the doctor said I could conceive. And I did!

Approximately two years after being discharged from the hospital, I was admitted there again, but this time for a much happier purpose. On February 21, 1989, I gave birth to a magnificent, wide-eyed baby boy with a heart-melting smile. You. Brandon Lee Spight. Our golden boy. Our little miracle. And everything was going to be all right in our world.

What I didn't realize, Bran, were other observers admiring similar traits in you. Here is what your Uncle Tommy wrote:

A few days ago, Gerald Woodward and I were talking about the standard to which Connie and Virgil raised Brandon and how they set the bar so high and operated with so much excellence. But when you think about it, that's how Connie and Virgil operated, in excellence. So what choice did or would Brandon have? From his relationships, artwork, and golf, the spirit of excellence permeated his activities as well.

Brandon was born at a stage in Virgil and Connie's lives when being good parents was their top priority. But when you think about it, were they only good parents, or did they do as Gerald Woodward suggested? Did they raise the bar? I contest that Connie and Virgil did raise the bar. They were excellent parents. For most of us, Brandon was not just Connie and Virgil's son. Brandon was and will always be someone I had a personal relationship with, someone I knew, the sidekick that was always there. If you saw Virgil and Connie, you saw Brandon. I recall the annual Bass Club banquets, and from the very beginning, Brandon was there, most times the only child present. He was always so proud to be there and witness Virgil win most of the trophies. He would also serve as Connie's dance partner as Virgil mingled with the fellas. Brandon evolved from a kid that accompanied his parents to the function to an independent teenager who drove himself. Wow, as Bass Club members, we were able to watch Brandon outgrow us!

Tommy Alston, family friend

3

GROWING UP BRANDON

Bran, the day you were born, Lisa called. Lisa has been my friend since childhood. Her mother, Ruth Fondren, and your granny were best friends and bowlers. They were two of the best African American female bowlers in Detroit. They bowled on the same team for many years. Lisa and her daughters, Kezia, Jillian, and Erica, were living in California at the time.

Lisa asked, "Are you in love yet?"

Was I ever! Immediately. Intensely. Eternally.

The first time I saw you—I mean, really looked at you—the maternity nurse brought you into my hospital room for your feeding. I saw those big, beautiful eyes and your lips that were already puckered in a sucking motion.

"Someone's hungry," the nurse cooed, looking at me.

At that moment, I understood to my core the profound bond that I had heard so much about before, a mother's love. No amount of daydreaming or imagining can prepare you for the all-encompassing and overwhelming wave of emotion you feel once you hold that tiny being in your arms and gaze into your baby's eyes for the first time. Once you were born, Brandon, it all became crystal clear. I don't believe I had ever given much thought to my purpose here on this earth. And for so long I had stopped imagining that a child would be in my future.

But upon your entry into this world, I knew you were my fulfillment, my destiny, and, without doubt, my purpose. Nothing before or since has meant more to me. Both your dad and I knew it. Brandon, I think even you knew it too. I loved being your mom.

While I was pregnant, there were many discussions pertaining to your name. None of which involved me. Your dad had decided that if you were a girl, your name was either going to be Jennifer Megan or Jennifer Margaret, Jennifer because he just liked the name and Margaret because that was the name of his great-aunt, the midwife at his birth, the woman who had been instrumental in raising him.

Your dad and my mom were always in competition about one thing or another, and she chimed in, "Well, if it's a boy, I'm going to name him!"

I kept thinking, *What about me? Does the baby's mother get a vote?*

Your granny wanted your name to be Brandon. She never explained why she picked that name, but I liked the name well enough, and your dad already had a namesake, Virgil Jr., from his previous marriage. Your dad gave his stamp of approval to Brandon, and we gave you Lee as a middle name, the same as your father's.

You were not so accepting! As you got older, you continually complained that Brandon was too common a name. "Mom," you would say, "there are Brandons everywhere!" I only wish I had had the forethought to name you Jackson after my dad. I think you and your granddad would have loved that!

In the fall of 1989, just six months after becoming a mother, I made the rather unorthodox decision to enter law school at Wayne State University. I considered delaying it, but your dad urged me to go. It sounds crazy to me today, but it made complete sense to me then. I didn't go to law school because I had cabin fever or needed an escape from the stressful new duties of motherhood.

Call me an overachiever, but I always enjoyed learning new things and the structure and goals of school. I had always intended to go to law school and had planned to enroll years earlier after graduating from Michigan State, but life took me down a different path.

All those years when I could have gone to law school—before I married Virgil and before I had you—I just kept putting it off. I believe, however, it was much better that I began when you were an infant rather than waiting until you became a toddler.

You were a good baby! Loving you came naturally. And caring for you was unexpectedly easy. We were lucky. You only cried when expressing the common needs of an infant. Because I knew my return to work was imminent and that I would start law school soon, I began training you at four months old to hold your own bottle. I'd place your tiny hands around it and then tip it just so, gradually pulling my hands away until you found a way to support it on your own. Your independence has always been very important to me.

Bran, sometimes I would wonder if you even noticed I was gone! I attended night classes, so when I came home, your dad had already fed and bathed you and was holding you in his arms, delaying bedtime so you and I could play or cuddle. Oftentimes you'd be sound asleep by the time I arrived home.

Other nights, you would be in your crib but only half-asleep, and you'd look up at me with those big eyes as if to say, "Who the heck are you?" Please know that this did not sit well with me as a new mother with her first child! I worried that you'd forget about me or not be close to me, and I loved and missed you so much while I was away in class or studying. But your dad never made me feel like I had made the wrong decision. Instead he'd give me words of support. "Don't you worry about it, Connie. Brandon's always going to love his mama." And your dad was right!

On one memorable occasion, upon my arrival home after working all day and attending classes in the evening, I walked into the door to find you wide awake! Your dad then proceeded to say, "Connie, Brandon can walk!"

My reaction was sadness because I was thinking, *Oh no, I missed a milestone!*

Noticing my regret, your dad said, "He hasn't walked yet, but I'm seeing signs that he's ready. I kept him up so you would see him walk for the first time."

Now my emotions were clashing with relief and excitement! We positioned ourselves so you had just enough room between us.

I then said, "Come here, Brandon," and your dad let you go.

You raised your arms as if you were a gymnast about to do an acrobatic flip, and you didn't walk, Bran. You trotted! It was wonderful and hilarious. I laughed and cried. But you knew I was enjoying it. You didn't stop. You careened toward me as we laughed. You turned around and propelled yourself toward Dad as you laughed hysterically, still with those little arms in the air. Typical you, Brandon! At just ten months old, you were performing for your audience.

Brandon, you were surrounded by so many relatives and friends who gladly stepped up to be part of your village. They were delighted by you, and because they stepped up to help take care of you, they made it possible for me to return to work as a Detroit police lieutenant and to earn my much-desired law degree.

At the home-based daycare in our neighborhood, operated by the wife of a Detroit police officer, you became the darling of their teenage daughters. On most days when we arrived at the end of the day, you were upstairs in their family room with the girls away from the common daycare area in the lower level.

As social as you were as a kid, you were totally comfortable playing for hours by yourself. Your Uncle Clyde, to his surprise, witnessed this on your first birthday. While family and friends were celebrating your first year in this world, you decided to slip away, crawl upstairs into your bedroom, and nestle yourself on the floor surrounded by your books and toys. Your Uncle Clyde followed you and decided to just sit and watch, amazed by your independence. By the way, you probably inherited part of your personality from your Uncle Clyde, so between your uncle and your dad, you were destined to be that guy who was the life of the party!

Brandon, you demonstrated a concern and care for others at an early age. When you were three and attending the Focus: HOPE Center for Children preschool, you impressed a staffer one day. You were outside on the playground when you stopped playing to take the new girl by the hand to show her where the restrooms were. And then you waited to guide her back to the playground!

Just think, a few months prior, you were going through potty training yourself. Let me tell you about how you learned to use the bathroom. When it came to potty training, the old folks kept telling me that boys were more difficult to train than girls. "You really have to be persistent with boys and make sure you sit them on the pot," they would say.

So who's the trainee here, the child or me? Since I was determined that you weren't going to train me, Bran, you and I had a serious talk. Being the exceptionally precocious toddler that you were, I figured, "Okay, he's got it." I concluded our little training session by telling you, "The next time you have to go to the potty, you have to let me know."

You replied very convincingly, "Okay, Mom, I will."

Of course it wasn't that easy. You avoided that potty like the plague! I would catch you hiding behind the couch doing your business or running to find me and desperately tugging on your soiled diaper or training pants yelling "Pot! Pot!" in that tone as if to say, "Okay, Mom, I'm telling you! I gotta go!" As much as that whole ordeal was cute at the time and I could barely contain my laughter, we clearly had not accomplished our goal!

So I decided to use a different approach. "Brandon, today you only get to watch *Sesame Street* (your favorite show) if you tell me when you have to use the potty as soon as you need to go. If you have an accident, no TV!"

You looked at me and nodded your head in agreement. And that day you were perfect! You told me when you had to go, you used your potty, and you got to watch your TV programs. I couldn't believe it at first, but then I patted myself on the back for being such an insightful, on-top-of-it mom and conquering this whole potty-training thing in a cinch.

That lasted for one day. The next day you reverted to doing it the Brandon way, hiding behind the couch. Now I was totally bewildered! We had the talk again. Then you asked if you could watch your favorite show on TV.

Slightly stunned, I replied, "No, Brandon, remember our talk: you use the potty, and then you get to watch TV."

I'll never forget your reply. "But Mommy," you said as innocently as any two-and-a-half-year-old could, "I used the potty yesterday!" Clearly I had failed to negotiate the duration of our contract.

By the time I finished law school, you obviously were tired of seeing me hovering over heavy textbooks to study. When I was writing my last law school paper, I had covered our library floor with open law books. I kept telling you it was the last paper I was going to write. After I turned in the paper, you found me in the library picking up the mess.

"No more books," you yelled. "You said you were done."

I had to reassure you that this was cleanup, not another paper.

I earned my law degree in December 1993, a semester early, when you were a four-year-old. Although I never practiced law, I am proud of this significant accomplishment. It was a life goal that I desired, achieved, and cherished. The understanding from my two guys, you and your dad, gave me strength to achieve that goal.

By this time, you had been attending Detroit Country Day

School for a year, one of the area's top private schools. Your dad insisted that he wanted you to go to "one of the best schools, if not the best school" in the area because he wanted you to have all the advantages in life he felt he didn't get. Country Day was in the affluent suburb of Birmingham, about twenty miles from our house. I was working in downtown Detroit at that time, while your dad was assigned to the Police Athletic League (PAL) on the northwest side of Detroit.

On most mornings, by the time I had driven you to school and then commuted thirty miles to police headquarters, I felt like I had driven across the state and back. I had to go into my office, close the door and collect myself, have a cup of coffee, and catch my breath before I could open the door and ask my clerk what was on the day's agenda.

It was a grueling schedule and a formidable trek in the wintertime, slogging through the snow and sliding on icy side streets ahead of the salt trucks. And Country Day never canceled school due to the weather. Never! I remember so many wintry mornings you would race downstairs all excited, look at the TV, and ask, "Mom, did the school close?" But every other school's name would scroll on the screen as closed, except yours. "Let's get ready to make that drive," I would reply.

Country Day had bus transportation, but that wasn't an option for me. Call me overprotective, cautious, or whatever you like. We chose to drive you to school, and the peace of mind was worth it.

By now, Brandon, your personality was evident to everyone. I wasn't surprised that you were outgoing and extremely vocal. While I was pregnant, I sat in your room-to-be and read books to you. As a baby, we talked to you as if you understood our every word. None of that baby talk! But what probably had the most influence on you were our family gatherings. They were always loud and demonstrative, everyone trying to outperform each other. "Quick-witted," your dad would always say of his kids. My brother, your

Uncle Clyde, was the same way, and so were my aunts, uncles, and cousins.

Brandon, you were our star at home. You eagerly entertained your dad and me at the dinner table. So when you started Country Day School at the age of three, accustomed to being the center of attention, you prided yourself in being the kid everyone loved, listened to, and followed. The only problem was that some of your teachers were not in awe of your intoxicating personality.

So when you were three years old, my years of advocating on your behalf began when I picked you up from school one afternoon. I drove to the pickup line, placed you in your rear car seat, and then heard your Pre-K3 teacher urgently calling me, "Mrs. Spight! Mrs. Spight!" I turned to see your teacher rapidly approaching the car, as you were persistently commanding me to drive away. "Go, Mom, go!"

I waited, of course, only to hear a complaint about you injuring another boy with a plastic knife. As I sat listening to what sounded like a description of a felonious assault, I felt my anger rise to what may have been an unacceptable level. So I decided to temporarily accept the teacher's description of the occurrence and delay comment. This was a Friday afternoon, so I politely informed her that I would discuss it with her on Monday morning.

As I drove off, Brandon, you immediately chimed in and told me what had happened. Apparently the kids in your class were engaging in an activity with Play-Doh when you and another boy started playfully sword-fighting with the plastic knives provided by the teacher.

"Mom, he scratched me too. You could just see his scratch better than mine."

So on Monday morning, being "Mom the Advocate," I arrived early to talk with the teacher. In a cool, calm tone, but as stern as I could be, I told her that I thought her response was overblown and that I was surprised she felt that play-fighting was unusual behavior for young children. I continued by suggesting that perhaps a plastic knife with ridges was not an acceptable tool for a three-year-old.

I wasn't naïve about who you were. I just didn't want to break your spirit. I was also sensitive to the fact that you were one of only two African-American boys in your grade at the time, at a private school that was predominantly Caucasian, and I was determined not to allow you to be singled out as a troublemaker. I used to tell my dad that your personality was a combination of Virgil and my brother Clyde all wrapped up in this little person that I had to raise. Why weren't you quiet like I was at that age? My dad would just laugh and assure me that I could handle it. Your pre-K4 teacher the following year was a welcome change.

I had the pleasure of being Brandon's Pre-K4 teacher from fall 1993 to spring 1994. Three particular thoughts come to mind as I close my eyes and think back about that little boy wonder.

First, oh, how he loved to build, always with a hard hat on. He loved Duplos and waffle blocks, but the wooden blocks were his favorite. The structures he built were fantastic. I would often remind him of our class rule to not build above his head. He would flash that sweet smile, bat those big brown eyes, nod his head, and reposition the towering blocks.

This brings me to my second thought, his beautiful brown eyes. I recall when he was sad or had been hurt, his eyes would well up, and then in no time, giant crocodile tears would come out and roll down his sweet cheeks. He was truly irresistible, both happy and sad! His boundless energy was apparent to all around him. His love of school, friends, and family was great.

This brings me to my third thought. Brandon was so happy and proud the days Mommy brought him to school. He was equally as excited the day Daddy brought him to school. However, when Granny picked him up, he was always so sweet and endearing to her that it warmed my heart. What a beautiful, loving boy with a family to

match. As I close my eyes right now, I envision him and Granny,
hand in hand, smiling down on us below.
With love,
Mrs. Michelle Novaco

Hey, Bran, do you remember your big sister, Diane, visiting you
at Country Day? I'm sure you do! Here's how that came about. On
one rare occasion, I picked you up from school. After your teacher
helped you into your car seat, she said she needed to speak with me.

She came around to my window and asked, "Mrs. Spight, does
Brandon have siblings?"

I responded, "Yes, he does."

As her body recoiled away from the car with an "I can't believe
I was wrong" look on her face, she simply responded, "Oh." I knew
she desired a full explanation, but I simply wished her a nice day.

As I was driving away, Bran, you piped up. "Mom, I told her I
had a big sister and big brothers, but she didn't believe me."

As it turns out, there was a class assignment for all the kids
to draw a picture of their family. Bran, you drew your little self
surrounded by six tall figures: your dad, me, and your four grown
siblings from Dad's first marriage. I guess that initiated the teacher
questioning your truthfulness.

Well, when Diane heard about this, she decided to make a
surprise visit to your school during your lunch hour. When you
saw her enter, you announced with pure joy, "That's my big sister!"

Your classmates were shocked, and one responded, "But she's
an adult!"

"She's still my sister!" you exclaimed.

Bran, your sister gained immense pleasure in corroborating your
story. To this day, she still enjoys recounting it, as if it happened
yesterday.

When your granny was still alive, she and your granddad loved
to pick you up after school. Your granny reveled in her status as a

Country Day grandmother. Your granny would tell anybody she thought might want to listen, "Oh, I have to go to Country Day now to get my grandson."

And when she was at Country Day, she relished seeing the children of Detroit's city officials or pro athletes there as your schoolmates. Brandon, she was so very, very proud that you were there. She was also intent on branding you, Brandon, as a Country Day student. After seeing so many kids wearing backpacks with the exclusive Country Day logo, she insisted that I get you one. "Brandon needs a backpack," she told me one day and for several days after.

"Brandon has a backpack, Ma," I told her.

"But it doesn't say Country Day on it! Oh, Connie, you've got to get him a Country Day backpack!"

"No," I said, "I don't. He's fine."

Granny insisted, "No, he's not. I'm going to go to the Country Day store and buy my grandson a backpack."

I had never been inside the Country Day store! I had no reason to step inside it; nor did I know where it was located. But the next day, off she went to get your backpack. When she stood at the checkout counter to pay for it, the clerk essentially told Granny no cash was needed. "Oh no, ma'am. This will just go onto Mr. and Mrs. Spight's account."

When I picked you up later at your grandparents' house, you were sporting a brand-new Country Day backpack. Your grandmother said, "By the way, it's going to show up on your account."

"My account?"

"Yes! They wouldn't take my money!"

Bran, I didn't even know we had a Country Day account. But sure enough, the school sent us the bill for your granny's gift.

The main reason we enrolled you in Country Day was for the academics, and we kept you there from pre-K (age three) through the sixth grade. Country Day was an impressive educational institution, but as a mom who experienced it right alongside you, there were also some challenges.

My greatest concern was that you were a young black male in a predominantly white school, and I didn't want that difference to negatively affect you. I wanted you to be well rounded as well as have pride in your black heritage. I also wanted you to look at people as people and like or dislike them for who they were, not for their outer coverings. My desire was fulfilled, Brandon, because you saw people as people, not as black, white, brown, or yellow. If you liked them, you considered them a friend.

Yet I remember at least one instance in which you received a painful reminder that things were not the same for you as they were for your classmates. You were a popular kid, Brandon. You prided yourself on being the kid everyone loved, listened to, and followed. You enjoyed being invited for playdates. But once when I picked you up from a classmate's house near Country Day, I noticed that you were quiet, almost sullen, not your usual upbeat self.

"How did it go with your friend today?"

"Fine," you mumbled.

"Did you have fun?"

"It was okay."

Something's not right here, I thought.

After not speaking for a very long time, you said, "Mom, do I have to go back over there again?"

"You don't," I told him. "Why don't you want to go back?"

He didn't answer. There was another uncomfortable silence. I didn't push. You'd always tell me at your own pace.

"Mom," you finally confessed, "he asked me how my parents could afford to send me to Country Day."

I was stunned. "Really? What did you say?"

"I didn't say anything. Why do you think he asked me that, Mom?"

I could feel the anger rising in me. I knew that the child

didn't come up with a question like that on his own. He may have overheard his parents or others discussing us, mixing gossip with veiled accusations. If they're Detroit cops and they can send their kid to a private school in the suburbs, they must be on the take, right? Skimming off the top? They've got to be crooked because there's just no other way to swing it on their public-servant salaries!

"Well, Bran," I said, trying to remain calm as I explained, "he doesn't know or understand our financial status. But obviously we are perfectly capable of sending you to Country Day. We aren't borrowing any money, we don't have any loans, and you're not getting any special consideration at school. So we can afford it."

I continued to explain to you that your dad was a man who plans far into the future, is methodical about long-term planning, and does whatever he needs to make his plans come true. Virgil was set on Country Day right after playing a round of golf at Oakland Hills. The headmaster at the time was in his foursome. Your dad was impressed with what he heard about the school and was determined that you attend one of the best schools in the area. As he put it, he wanted to make sure that you "started the race from the starting line, not from the back of the pack."

We knew the cost of tuition, so we started saving a year before you were enrolled. From that point forward, we continued that account, the Brandon school account, so that every year we were prepared to pay your tuition.

Our friends used to joke, "Connie, doesn't it cost more to go to Country Day than it did to attend Michigan State University?"

But we didn't care. Even though I cringed when we wrote the check—even more so as the tuition increased—that's what we elected to do. Your education was worth it to us.

At dinnertime, you were always eager to share the school day's events with us. But there were times adding your verbal contributions were challenging. It was easy—perhaps too easy— for your dad and me to bring our work home with us from police headquarters. Many nights at the dinner table, while we talked about our respective commands and administrative matters, you would jump into our conversation suddenly and yell, "No more police talk!" That jolted us sufficiently to turn to you and ask, "So, Brandon, what did you do today?"

I do believe though that hearing all that police talk and coming to understand what we did for a living had a major impact on you, Bran. It molded and developed you in ways that we didn't anticipate. Indeed I think it helped form you into a smart, successful, and charming negotiator.

Dad and I often talked about how to help our officers prepare for promotion interviews. We provided them with appropriate techniques to score well, such as making eye contact with everyone in the room; answering questions thoroughly but concisely; and confidently engaging with their interviewers.

We didn't know you were absorbing valuable knowledge from our cop-shop talks until you went to Space Camp in Huntsville, Alabama. As a Country Day fifth-grader, you were appointed captain of your squad. I asked as to how you acquired such an important responsibility. Brandon, you explained your appointment this way, "I just interviewed the way you tell your officers."

My parents didn't have a formal wedding or reception. They were married March 16, 1946, at Detroit City Hall. So we hosted a fiftieth-anniversary party at Breithaupt Center in Detroit for my parents on March 16, 1996, and gave them the wedding and celebration they never had. You were seven years old, and you were dashing in a little tuxedo as the ring bearer. Since you always had something to say, you demonstrated your talents with great flourish as the co-master of ceremonies with your dad.

After the wedding ceremony and the exchange of vows, the reception began. You actually opened the festivities, remember? You confidently took the microphone, introduced yourself, and welcomed the guests to the event. You weren't shy in the least.

"This is the wedding celebration for my grandparents, Charles and Quincy Jackson," you announced, "and I'll be your master of ceremonies for the evening. And now, to help me with this task, here is Virgil Spight, my dad!"

Then Virgil took the podium and introduced a succession of guests, each of whom shared memories or expressed warm regards to your granny and granddad. After a while though, you grew restless and sidled up to me.

"Mom," you complained, "Dad's had more mike time than me!"

"Really?"

"Yeah! He's been up there way longer than me!"

"Okay. You want the mike?"

"Yeah, Mom!"

I went up to the podium and whispered to your dad, who then called you back up to the stage and handed you the mike. You stayed alongside him for the rest of the evening, comfortable and confident in the spotlight. I watched with tremendous admiration. I wasn't anything like that when I was that age, Bran.

Bran, your grandparents were so proud of you!

Just a few months after the wedding celebration, your granny became ill. You and your granny were so incredibly close. You teased and joked with her as well, but she never doubted your love for her. During her illness, you truly showed your sensitive side. I don't think I was ever prouder of you than I was during her final months. She had become bedridden, and we were caring for her at her home.

Every day when you came home from school, you would go directly into her room to do your homework. You took private violin lessons for a couple years, and you were still playing then. You would play it for her. You talked to her, told her all about your day, held her hand, and gazed into her eyes.

Eventually she stopped talking … to everyone but you. My attempts to engage her in conversation were futile. And you'd gently nudge me to stop trying.

"She doesn't feel like talking, Mom," you'd say. You were connected to her in a way that no one else but the two of you shared.

While your granny was ill, your granddad had to relinquish his duties picking you up from school. Your granny passed on February 5, 1997. You were seven years old. After she passed, your granddad asked your dad if he could resume chauffeur duties. He asked, "Can I have my job back?"

That summer, you came to us and announced that you did not want to go to summer camp that year.

"Well, why not?" I asked.

"Because my granddad needs me," you replied. "I think he's going to be lonely without Granny. He won't have anyone to be with him."

You truly loved your granddad! On most days when you said his name, it sounded more like "Gretta" than "Granddad." Your Uncle Carl became acutely aware of this when you called to speak to your grandfather and three times your Uncle Carl said you had the wrong number!

"Mom," you exclaimed, "I'm calling Gretta, and Uncle Carl,

at least it sounds like Uncle Carl, keeps saying I've got the wrong number."

"Really?" I questioned because it wasn't until I called and talked to my brother that I even paid attention to the fact that your affectionate name for your grandfather sounded like Gretta.

Your Uncle Carl got quite a laugh from that. By the way, Bran, you would be proud to know that your Uncle Carl is quite computer savvy and spends a significant portion of his day searching the web. So all those hours you spent with him did not go in vain.

You went to my parents' house every day that summer of 1997, and I think it truly helped my father with his grief journey and the loneliness of being without his wife after fifty-one years of marriage. You were such a special kid, Brandon, loving and wise beyond your years. You gave your granddad what we all need when we lose a loved one, a reason to move on, to be engaged, to continue with purpose.

Remember when your Grandma Spight grew ill? We were once again taking turns caring for a family member. You and I were assigned Fridays after school. While I prepared a meal, you would entertain your grandmother, and she would look at you with such amazement. We loved your sensitivity and compassion for others. So when you proclaimed to me during one of our talks that you respected women, I didn't question your veracity.

Your Uncle Clyde and I often balked at our mother's wisdom. We responded with rolled eyes or know-it-all attitudes when she imparted her knowledge. But as adults we have often confessed, "Ma told us that!" and "We didn't believe her, but it was the truth!"

Your granny would say, "Children understand much more than adults give them credit" and "Always answer your child's questions no matter how uncomfortable it makes you." That advice resonated with me, so when your granny's health was failing, I explained her illness to you and taught you how to dial 911 and tell the operator that your granny needed help in case of an emergency. I had no doubt that you were prepared to handle the situation if it presented itself, that is, as I later discovered, if the emergency involved your granny.

About a year after your granny passed, an emergency occurred that shocked you into a state of panic, erasing the earlier lessons you had learned. You and I were upstairs after returning from the bookstore. You, of course, were browsing through your books in an effort to decide which one to read first when we heard a noise that sounded like someone stumbling and then several loud thumps and crashing noises coming from downstairs.

We ran downstairs to find your dad on the floor, looking as if he'd suffered a stroke. As I attempted to lift him to a sitting position, I simultaneously instructed you to call 911. You picked up the phone but stood frozen with an expression of absolute horror on your face.

I continued to attempt to communicate with your dad. "Virgil, can you hear me?" No response. I repeated, "Bran, call 911 and hand me the phone."

"What, Mom ... do what ... what's wrong with Dad?" you cried.

Without further hesitation, I took the phone from you and made the call while using my body to support your dad. Your dad was incapacitated, and so were you! At the time, I was the commanding officer of communications. Upon identifying myself to the 911 operator and requesting EMS immediately, the operator asked, "Commander, is that you?"

Jesus, I thought, *not you too!*

"Yes, it's me. Please send EMS!"

EMS arrived just as your dad was returning to consciousness. But by then, the entire police community had heard over the radio transmissions about your dad's situation. The executive duty officer, a sergeant from the 12th Precinct, and several other concerned officers all seemed to arrive at once. As much as I was elated to see them, your dad was embarrassed by the attention and professed to be perfectly fine.

With my explanation and the observation of the technicians, however, we concurred that he required a hospital visit. Your dad, in all his pride, insisted on walking out to the ambulance. He would not be carried out on a stretcher. Your dad's diagnosis was never determined, but from that day forward, you had a protective eye on him.

On a lighter note, when your dad retired from the Detroit Police Department in 1999, you were front and center at his retirement party in January 2000. You were on the dais welcoming the guests and introducing the master of ceremonies. Here is a portion of what you said:

Good evening, ladies and gentlemen. Welcome to the retirement celebration of former Commander Virgil Spight. My name is Brandon Spight. I think most of you know who I am. I see a lot of familiar faces, but for those of you who do not know who I am, I'll tell you.

I am the youngest child of former Commander Virgil Spight. I'm eleven years old, or should I say almost eleven since my birthday is Monday, February 21. I attend Detroit Country Day School, and I'm in the fifth grade.

But we aren't here to talk about me. We're here to celebrate the retirement of my dad. He has retired from the Detroit Police Department after thirty-five years. And I am especially happy to see him retire since this will give him more time to spend with me on the golf course, even though this will also give him more time to yell at me. Just kidding, Dad, but you do tell me to stop moving my head a lot on the golf course! All kidding aside, I am very proud of my dad and extremely happy to be here celebrating his retirement.

Bran, you were proud of your dad and enjoyed travels together, which were often memorable. You delighted in coming back and telling me everything you saw, did, and felt. Once after going to the store with your dad, you walked in the house and announced, "Mom, I don't want to be cute. I want to be fine."

With an eyebrow raised, I asked, "Oh really? Why is that?"

"Well," you explained, "there was this lady at the store, and she came up to the car window and said to Dad, 'I just want to tell you that you are fine.'"

"Oh, this lady said that to your dad, did she? And what did your dad say?"

Your dad wasn't happy with your talkative nature that day! But you know, I think in a way that brief, frivolous encounter made a profound impression on you. From that point on, you were determined to be fine, just like your dad.

At an early age, it was determined you would require braces. It wasn't a revelation since your dad had a gap between his two front teeth before it was corrected. I could see your gap even though you still had baby teeth. Later when it became obvious that your sight wasn't 20/20 and the ophthalmologist said you were nearsighted, I wasn't surprised at that either. I started wearing glasses when I was twelve. You didn't welcome wearing braces or glasses. From the start, you couldn't wait to get out of them! I thought you were cute in either or both, but as far as you were concerned, there was no way you could be fine!

After your persistent urging, I finally agreed to contact lenses when you were fifteen. As we were driving to the ophthalmologist's office, I kept thinking, *Oh, Lord, why are we doing this?* I'd heard horror stories about kids leaving contacts in too long and getting an eye infection or worse.

You couldn't leave the office until you learned how to put them in yourself. *Oh no,* I thought. *We're going to be here all day with this boy!* I mean, I don't wear contact lenses because I cannot successfully stick a finger in my eye to put them in.

Pop! Pop! You put in both lenses on the very first try! The nurse said you had to do it a second time. You were out in minutes.

"He's a pro," the nurse said.

"Okay, Mom, I'm ready," you said, looking at me with that captivating grin. "Can we go now?"

And you did look fine!

4

GETTING INTO THE SWING

Looking back at it now, Bran, I wonder if you were trying to prepare me for your death long before you left us. So many times you told me, "Mom, you need to video me playing golf." I finally gave in and bought a video camera. But it was so big and bulky to carry around the course that I just didn't use it much. I regret that.

My reluctance to take the camera out of its case would prompt your persistent warning, "Mom, you're gonna miss me when I'm gone!" Of course, you were referring to going away for college, but now I wonder if God were giving me a sign. Even without the video replay, I have vivid images of you playing golf.

Your relationship with golf started while I was pursuing my law degree at Wayne State, when your dad took care of you most weekdays, late afternoons, and evenings. Your dad was simply amazing in terms of supporting me and being there with you. Frequently after he got off work, your dad would stop by your granny's house or the babysitter to pick you up. Then he'd drive straight to the golf range, with you in tow, to get in some practice.

Your dad didn't take up the sport of golf until he was forty-three. But once he did, it was as if he were determined to make up for lost time! Obsessed by the game, he'd play or practice any time the opportunity presented itself. Whether he was on the driving range or putting green, he would take you along and plant you nearby in your car seat. You were out of harm's way, of course, but Dad made sure you could see him practicing his swing.

Dad says you followed his every move. "Never once did he cry," your dad says about you. You'd happily sit there and watch intently. The same was true if your dad were in the basement, working on his chip shots. Your gaze was fixed on your dad. You never tried to chase the balls.

Even before you could hold a club, your dad strategized how to get you ready for golf. He would lift you up from the ground as you held onto his hands with just two of your fingers. "Helps Brandon develop a strong grip," your dad would say. Obviously you weren't idly watching; you were studying your dad's swings intently and taking mental notes.

Here's why we know this to be true: When you were old enough to stand on your own, your dad had a little right-handed golf club made especially for you. You're right-handed, but when your dad gave you the club to use, you wouldn't swing it from your right side. Instead you imitated your dad and swung from the left! Virgil is also right-handed, but he is ambidextrous and plays golf as a left-hander. "It gives me greater hand-eye coordination," your dad says, "and a smoother swing." And, as usual, you wanted to be smooth like your dad!

"You see, Virgil," I reminded him, "kids do as you do!"

You wanted to play left-handed because your point of reference was your dad, your only exposure to the world of golf at that time. After seeking advice from a respected golf teaching professional, your dad gave in and had a left-handed club cut down to your size. Nearly everyone who ever saw you or your dad play golf just assumed you both were left-handed. In Virgil's case, they still do.

Before you were born, your dad took winter golf trips every February to Florida. These trips were normally scheduled at the end of February during winter break to accommodate the schoolteachers in the traveling group. Your birthday, February 21, usually fell during that golf week, so we grew accustomed to celebrating your special day either before your dad left or after he returned.

My mother would say, "Oh, that's not going to last. Brandon will change all that."

And sure enough, when you got a little older and your dad started talking about his winter golf trip, you would look at him with those big brown eyes and say, "Dad, you're going away on my birthday again?" As my mother prophesied, the dates for the winter trip were revised so your dad could be home on your birthday!

You followed in your father's golf spikes, embracing the game with every ounce of the passion, precision, and dedication that your dad displayed. You admired your dad so, and you took to his instruction and advice like a baby tadpole takes to water. And you were good too. Your dad could tell right away, and as Dad pointed out certain things to me, so could I.

Your dad has always been a terrific athlete. He played touch football with the City of Detroit team, ran track with the police department team, and played for the Michigan Chronicle fast-pitch softball league. When the Detroit Police Department sent him to the FBI Academy, Virgil broke the push-up and sit-up records. He excelled athletically and didn't shy away from letting you know it.

But he was crazy about golf even before you were born, and once you shared that passion with him, it made him even more passionate about the sport. Your dad would marvel at your smooth swing. "Brandon never seems like he's swinging hard." Your swing was a blend of lithe grace and controlled power.

But your dad didn't want you to play golf just because he played it. He entered you in every sport in which you showed even a passing interest because he didn't want to deny you the opportunity to discover some other talent.

You played soccer and later baseball. Your baseball experience started with t-ball. It was quite comical during that first season watching all the boys in the outfield (including you) running after the ball. You played baseball a few years, progressing to coach pitch and player pitch. Your baseball coach took a liking to you and praised your hitting ability. But there was one baseball season when you came back the coach wondered why you were racking up consecutive strikeouts in a game.

"Spight, what's going on with you?" the coach shouted. He continued studying you at the plate and spotted the big difference from the previous seasons, much to his dismay.

"I know the problem!" he exclaimed while looking over at your dad. "That's a golf swing! You're trying to play baseball like golf! You can't do that!" He then called you over to the side. After hammering a stick into the ground, the coach told you, "Now swing at the top of that stick."

You kept looking at me as if to say, "Please make him stop!" However humiliating that exercise may have been, you got a hit that day. No more strikeouts.

In between baseball seasons, you received professional golf lessons. Because of your natural ability, enhanced by pro tips, you could hit a golf ball a very long way at a very young age. Virgil often took you to an indoor golf dome in Madison Heights, Michigan, to practice, where you caught the eye of the owners when you were about six years old. Over time the two brothers who owned the facility marveled over your swing and the distance you could generate and started making bets with other golfers.

"Hey, you see that little guy over there?" one brother would begin. "I'll bet you five bucks he can hit the ball to the back of the dome."

"C'mon! There's no way that kid can hit a ball that far!" the unsuspecting golfer would typically reply. "You're on!"

It was, of course, a sucker bet: You could tattoo the back of that dome wall with ease. Once they collected the winnings, the owners would hand over the money to your dad as you looked on. Virgil let you save the $10 or so betting money.

In full honesty, Bran, you and I know it wasn't always "easy breezy," as I recall your early tournament days on the Meijer Junior Tour. It was your first tournament, and you hit a ball out of bounds. Then after another wayward shot, penalties mounted, resulting in an eleven on that hole. That hole had a negative effect on the rest of the round. The sight of your name close to the bottom of the leaderboard deflated your usual upbeat spirit. On the way home, you repeatedly cried that maybe you weren't good enough. I promptly squashed that notion, assuring you that even the pros have mishaps on the course.

Your dad was determined to improve your game and level of confidence, so he encouraged you to continue with the Meijer Tour. You also traveled to New York with the Detroit Police Athletic League at the age of ten, attended the First Tee National Academy at Kansas State University July 12–19, 2003, and later competed on the PowerBilt Golf Tour.

Bran, remember how your dad would shake coins in his pocket during your putting stroke? That would totally unnerve you. "Mom," you would protest quietly to me, "did you see what Dad did?" Even I thought that was cruel, but Virgil insisted it would improve your focus and concentration abilities.

You and your dad entered your first father-son tournament when you were about seven. It was at Palmer Park, and the two of you were paired with another father and his ten-year-old son. Your dad thrashed his counterpart with ease. But the ten-year-old, although narrowly, beat you. You were angry and nearly inconsolable! You cried and ranted about it for hours.

"I know one thing," your dad often says when he tells this story, "we never lost a father-son tournament again."

Your swing dazzled your dad's golf buddies. However, your dad's friend, Harvey Taylor, told your dad he would never play golf with you because you were just a kid. One day I dropped you off at a golf course after school to meet your dad and he was playing with Harvey that day. Harvey didn't expect much from you. But when he saw your swing, he realized it was not the swing of a kid and that he had completely underestimated your talent.

Harvey often joked, "I thought you were going to twist your narrow ass into the ground every time you hit a drive because you had so much power."

Our neighbor Ken Jones told us he once asked you if you could beat your dad at golf.

"Every now and then," you replied.

"Well then, will you let your father beat you every now and then once you get older?"

"No," you politely answered.

You had it: charisma, confidence, attitude, unrelenting commitment to grow and improve, and pure raw talent. Young people used to call it "swag." Whatever it was, it revealed itself in a singular focus and intensity that one rarely sees in boys so young.

Folks couldn't help but notice. Gloria Reynolds experienced it firsthand.

Duel on a Summer's Day

It was a beautiful summer day with just enough time to play nine holes.
Friends on the tee, what a pleasant surprise.
They were all smiles and sparkly eyes, a proud father and son.
My goodness, Brandon, look how you've grown!
We began a friendly game, Brandon and I from the forward tees.
One, two, three, four holes go quickly by. Can I really be down by a stroke, maybe two?
It seemed the friendly game had changed.
The sparkle in his eyes and the ever-so-slight smile at the corners of his mouth were
Familiar, like a reflection.
Whose son? You could see a little mom, a little dad.
He's engaged, he's focused—and believes he can win!
Like a tiger on the prowl he's coming after me.
Oh no! I couldn't be beaten by a ten-year-old? Never!
The duel is on!

For five holes, the battles rage. Game face on, we struggle. Every stroke matters.
Focus, intensity—we're even. I'm up, I'm down,
I scramble, I escape!
Another familiar look, like a reflection, I hate to lose!
It was a beautiful summer day, a cherished memory.
Gloria Reynolds, coworker

As you entered your teens, your dad regularly took you on his weekend golf outings, joining a dozen buddies he had teed off with on Sundays since long before you were born. The guys played for money. Each player put money in the "skin pot," and unbeknownst to me, you were part of it too! The amount could be up to $10 per player. Whatever the amount, your dad would put in for himself and you. After the completion of eighteen holes, the pot was divided between the golfers who scored par or better on certain holes.

Despite your age, you were regularly winning a skins pot. It was just a matter of time, Bran, before you flashed your wad of bills in my face and boasted about your winnings. You couldn't help yourself! What son doesn't want to impress his mother with his accomplishments?

"The blabbermouth is so honest that he can't keep nothing quiet," your dad complained, "especially from his mom."

Your dad tried to explain to me that betting was part of the golf culture and that he didn't expect you to win. I told your dad it was all right to bring you with him on his Sunday rounds, but by no means was he to put you in the skins game! Betting for money is a very bad precedent to instill in one as young as you were, and your dad knew better. I told your dad to never let you be a part of the skins game again.

Bran, your disappointment and displeasure were evident. And every Sunday you reminded me of your displeasure by eagerly displaying your scorecard and calculating the amount of money you could have won.

It wasn't just that you didn't like losing; nobody enjoys the taste of defeat. You absolutely despised losing, Bran, be it at golf, video games, games with the family, anything! More so than anyone I've ever known. At a much younger age when you and I played Monopoly, you cried if I bought Boardwalk or Park Place.

If you and a friend were drawing pictures, afterward you'd ask me, "Which one is the best, Mom?"

"They're both good," I would reply.

"No, Mom, you have to pick which is better!"

Your competitiveness and confidence were hallmarks of your game. One of your University of Detroit Jesuit classmates, Nick

Hammer, witnessed many firsthand examples of your utter hatred of losing. No matter the occasion, Nick said you played to win.

"After our sophomore year, I was playing in a fundraiser for a summer camp," Nick recalls. "There were probably eight foursomes of very casual golfers, and they needed another man, so I asked Brandon to come out and play with me. Coming down the stretch, it appeared we were close to being in the lead. Brandon would not talk to me for the last three holes! He just kept walking beside me saying, 'You gotta focus. You gotta win this hole!' And I'd say, 'What are you talking about? No one cares!'"

But Brandon, you cared, and you wouldn't relent. "No," you told Nick, "I'm walking next to you because this is serious!"

You were born with a blazing competitive fire. Nick was unaware that this level of competitiveness had been transferred to you from your dad. Your dad always had a desire to win, and he sparked it in you too. Your dad would even challenge you to races going up the stairs in the house.

"I wouldn't let him win," your dad said, "and then Brandon would say, 'Let's do it again.'"

The three of us often had our own tournament play. It was you and I against your dad. During one of our first tournaments, I was unsure which club to use. I asked your dad for advice, and he literally stood there looking at me as if I had not spoken.

Brandon, you enlightened me, saying, "Mom, we're competing. He's not going to help you."

Your dad embraced your talent. He rejoiced in it. He often said he wanted to "make himself a Tiger," as in the legendary Tiger Woods. He bought Earl Woods' book, *Raising a Tiger*, to get tips on how to raise a golf pro.

For your part, you would often proclaim—not completely in jest—that you intended to be "the first golfer to make the pro tour from Palmer Park," the City of Detroit–owned public course about a mile from our house, which you affectionately nicknamed

"P-Square." You started calling it that after a school team golf trip. You told me your teammates asked, "Hey, Spight, what country club do you belong to?"

"P-Square," you proudly responded.

You initially golfed at Palmer Park with your dad, then with your dad and me, and sometimes just you and me. Later I would drop you off to play with your friends, or you would drive yourself there. Over the years, employees who worked the course and golfers who patronized it got to know you well. You went so often that it was not unusual for your dad and me to be enjoying a round of golf and suddenly see you approaching in a golf cart, grinning from ear to ear, as if you had caught us sneaking behind your back.

I was very involved in transporting you to every golf tournament and practice, Bran. I enjoyed watching you and carrying your Gatorade and food to place at the turn (after nine holes of an eighteen-hole round).

We've kept the golf balls you saved and marked every time you reached a personal best: the first time you broke 100 in a round; your first eagle (August 1, 2000) on the fourth hole at Palmer Park; your first hole-in-one, 145 yards with an 8-iron at Rackham (July 31, 2003); and your second hole-in-one at Rouge Park (May 17, 2006).

As I recall, your first hole-in-one nearly gave me a heart attack. After retiring from the police department in October 2000, I took a year off and then became a real estate agent in September 2001. I was showing houses on the east side one day when you called me. I couldn't answer the phone right away, but I was also thinking, *He's on the golf course. Why is he calling?*

A few minutes lapsed, and you called again. When I called back, there was no answer. "What the …?"

After apologizing to my clients, I got in my car and sped from the east side of Detroit about twenty-two miles away to Rackham Golf Course in Huntington Woods. I was thinking all kinds of crazy: "Oh God, he got hit in the head by a golf ball!" When I arrived, I dashed into the clubhouse. I was relieved to find you upright with no visible blood or injuries and signing some forms.

"Mom, I got a hole-in-one!" you screamed in excitement.

Your dad bought you a hole-in-one necklace. It was just like his. Every time you stepped on a course afterward, you wore that necklace.

When you weren't playing, you were practicing. You and your father would practice chipping and putting endlessly in our basement during the winter months. You always wanted your dad to force me to practice too. "How come you're not making Mom practice?" you questioned your dad. Your dad jokes that you and he would often shame me into joining the basement practice sessions, egging me on with the taunt that I couldn't even hit a decent chip on the practice mat.

As you know, Bran, I didn't exactly take to the game right away. Did I learn how to play? What choice did I have? If I wanted to spend time with you and be part of our family, I had to pick up a club!

Our vacations centered around golf. We traveled to Florida, Tennessee, Las Vegas, Hawaii, and the famed oceanside Pebble Beach course in California. Our last day on a Florida trip, you begged to ride with me in the golf cart. Typically I always rode alone so you and your dad could share a cart and talk shots and strategy, even as you vigorously competed against each other. You went into this last round, however, tied for the Spight Family Vacation Best Player Award. But, Bran, you knew that if you rode with your father, he would try to play mind tricks with you and throw you off your game. Oh, you two were so competitive!

"Please, Mom," you pleaded, "let me ride with you! I gotta win to be the champ. I can't let Dad get in my head!"

Well, after some token resistance, of course I gave in. You rode with me, and you beat your dad that day. Very few things on earth made you happier than defeating your father. It made your dad very proud too, although he wouldn't tell you.

Our Hawaii trip when you were ten or eleven was memorable on several fronts, including the flight on which you were the only person with their reading light because you were so engrossed in your Harry Potter book while everyone else slept or on the cruise ship when the kids would stop me to introduce themselves and then ask, "Where's Brandon?" Or how I made you check in every hour and you surprisingly obliged or how your granddad made friends with the ladies on the tours while we played golf.

But mostly, what I tease your dad about was how he changed the course he had planned to play one day. Bran, you and I were doing our customary shopping in the clubhouse while your dad checked in and paid for the round. As you began looking at souvenir postcards, I heard you say, "Dad, I can't wait to play this hole. Look, it's an island green!"

Your dad cut his eyes at me and whispered, "We're not playing that course."

That was just fine with me because I was intimated by the photo! And, Bran, you know you always said I never saw water I didn't hit my ball in. However, regardless of my trepidation, your dad was determined to give you what you wanted! So unbeknownst to you, your dad changed the course so you could play the three-par island green hole. You and Dad landed your tee shot on the green and parred the hole, while I … well, you know where my ball landed!

I'm sure you recall our trip to Pebble Beach during your winter break in 2005, another golfing experience your dad wanted for you! You were having an exceptional round. Your tee shot on the last hole was long and straight. A birdie on that hole was in your sights. As you approached your ball to hit your second shot across the water, a wedding party in fancy clothing proceeded to walk across the grounds, causing you to wait until they cleared the fairway.

While they paraded across the fairway, you peered at them in shock, commenting, "Mom, are you kidding me?"

After the wedding party cleared the fairway, you approached your ball to hit the second shot, which went "splash" into the water! Totally annoyed, you knew that birdie was no longer possible.

The golf courses we played would ordinarily be insignificant to me, but discovering this three-inch-by-six-inch yellow piece of paper printed in your handwriting tugged at my heart:

GOLF
Spyglass: Fri: 1:40
Pebble Beach: Sat: 11:10
Spanish Bay: Sun: 10:30

On a trip to Las Vegas, we were privileged to have a caddie for the first time, remember? You and I loved the assistance. It felt like such a luxury! It took me several holes to remember to hand the caddie my club after a shot or ask him which way the greens were breaking that day, but not you! You fell right into the routine, conferring with the caddie about the course layout and pin placements as if you'd been playing pro golf for years. You were in your bliss! Your dad wanted nothing to do with the caddie, and you couldn't understand why, but that certainly didn't diminish your enjoyment. What you didn't know, Bran, was that your dad just enjoyed watching you and anticipating the years to come.

At every tournament you participated in, your dad spent considerable time observing your young competitors on the golf range. Ever wonder why you two were always at Carl's Golfland buying you new clubs? Your dad often made excuses by indicating you had outgrown your old clubs. Let me tell you, Brandon, most often it was because he noticed another young man hitting the ball well, inquired about the club he was using, and then turned to me and said, "I'm getting Brandon that driver" or "I'm getting Brandon those irons."

So as a thirteen-year-old, when you asked your dad to buy you a

$300 Scotty Cameron putter, he pretended to put a few parameters on the purchase. But I knew it was as good as yours.

"That's what the pros use," he told you.

"When you finish under par, I'll get you the club," Dad said, turning it into a challenge.

Two days later, Bran, you shot sixty-nine at Palmer Park. Challenge conquered!

"That was the happiest $300 I ever spent," your dad said.

Your dad uses that putter to this day. He replaces clubs all the times, but not your Scotty Cameron. Ask him about it, and he'll reply, "It's in my bag now, and I will never replace it."

Many times, we went golfing by ourselves, just you and me. And I think you already know this, Bran, but my absolute most memorable and enjoyable times on the golf course were the times when it was just the two of us. I was amazed when you would approach a chip shot on the side of a green and confidently say to me, "Mom, I'm going to chip this in." You never missed that shot with me. We kept score, and you always beat me. But I always left feeling like a winner too.

Bran, I think of you every day, even when I don't speak your name out loud. But I think of you even more while I'm playing golf. I couldn't play the Palmer Park course for a long time after you passed because, after all, that was your course, your P-square country club. I continue to play to this day, mostly with your dad. I try my best to improve my game every time out, even though you would tell me that I still don't practice enough. And I know you're right. But I play for you, Brandon. I play for you.

WHO I AM AND WHO I PLAN TO BECOME

My name is Brandon Spight. I am thirteen years old, and I attend U of D High School and Academy. My favorite classes are gym, science, and English. My favorite teachers are Mr. Slaughter, Mrs.

Rhea- Johnson, and Mrs. McIntyre. I feel that I am a very outgoing person. I enjoy socializing with friends and enjoy myself. Sometimes I can get out of control and begin to talk too much. That's where my problem lies. Over the years I have been in school, I have had some problems with teachers or even with my peers. I have gotten detentions and suspensions, and on many occasions I have had to speak with teachers, before school, after school, and after classes. Now I am not saying this to brag because of course this is not something to brag about, not at all. This is something that I am going to have to work on to change because the older I get, the more ridiculous it seems for me to be getting in trouble for the same things, year after year.

Faith-wise, I feel I am a faithful Christian, although I do not go to church every Sunday. That is something that I regret not doing, and so do my parents. I plan to go to church the older I get so I can learn about God and Jesus. I really enjoy religion class because like I said before, I want to learn more because as far as I am concerned, I do not know enough.

I am also a very loyal person. Right now and most likely always, my family is going to be the most important thing in my life. I love everyone in my family, and I will do anything for them. My parents are the leaders on the two sides of the family, and they are teaching me to take on responsibility head-on because someday I will be the leader of both families. That is why I feel so ready to take on the responsibility already because my parents do so well. It is great seeing them being able to handle problems in the family and eventually solve them.

When I get older, or as many people say, grow up, I want to be a kind, caring person who looks to help others before thinking of himself. I want to be the good guy, never the bad guy. I also hope I am as ready as I think to take on a responsibility, like taking care of my family when I get to be the respectable age. Not just my family on my mother and father's sides, but my own. I am hoping to be a father someday, and I hope I can set a good example for them. I also hope to have a promising career, but before all of this, I plan to go to college. College is very important to me and my parents as well. I hope to get a full-ride scholarship either for golf or academics. I really don't know what could make my parents happier. They have sent me to very good schools and spent so much money on golf equipment and golf lessons that I figure I ought to do something productive with it. So basically I hope I do well in my life to come. I certainly have the background for it.

That is who I am and who I plan to become. I hope you enjoyed reading about it.

This is Who I Am
by Brandon Spight, age 14

My name is Brandon.
I am loud and sociable.
I'm one of the best freshmen golfers,
But I am far more capable.
I want to be like Tiger
And play in the pros.
I want to be rich and wealthy
And wear the best clothes.
I want to dine like the stars
In all the finest restaurants.
Eat crab and other seafood
Or anything else I want.
I like music too.
I like the beat of the drums
and the flow of rappers.
I occasionally enjoy the smooth sound of R&B singers.
My eyes are brown, my hair is black,
And my favorite color is blue.
I'm sure all of you have a favorite color.
Maybe it's blue too.
I like to consider myself a leader.
I'm different from all the rest.
I love my life and won't change a thing.
I am indeed truly blessed.

5

BRANDON MAKES A STATEMENT

When I made my decision to become proficient in the game of golf, I didn't realize it would require me to live as a chameleon.

The older I became, I realized the sport I loved was golf. I have played this game since the age of three, despite enduring racist attitudes. These attitudes continue to be apparent when I walk through the golf course parking lot or step onto the first tee. The looks that people give me when I swing the club could burn a hole through a wall. However, after I hit a good shot, the look of astonishment is far more satisfying. I have learned to play through the looks, attitudes, and racist comments. I gained respect by posting good scores.

From Brandon's personal statement on college applications

What power you unleashed, Bran, both on and off the golf course! Brandon, you juggled expectations in the different worlds you traversed. You were not the son of local, well-known celebrities or Fortune 500 senior executives, and yet you had the ability to constantly adapt as though you possessed an inherent familiarity with that world.

In your preschool and elementary years at Country Day, you

were one of a handful of African Americans in the lower school. In our city neighborhood, even though it was an upper-middle-class neighborhood, you were taunted sometimes for preferring golf over basketball or football and for attending a suburban private school.

From pre-K through sixth grade, you attended Country Day and found friendship, academic excellence, and a measure of acceptance. I know you expected to stay there until you walked across the stage in your high school cap and gown. But the time came for a change.

I wanted you to experience a diverse, inclusive environment. We wanted a school closer to home, one that reflected our neighborhood as well as the larger Detroit area. We visited University of Detroit Jesuit High School and Academy (UDJ). We were impressed by the academic curriculum, the spiritual teachings and components, and the all-boy environment. We felt you could benefit from not being distracted by girls every school day. Your dad thought that being in a male-only environment at UDJ would compel you to concentrate on your studies and golf game, especially your golf game! And your dad was impressed that the school required its students to give back to the community through outreach programs. We enrolled you in UDJ for the seventh grade.

At first, you weren't buying in about attending an all-boy school. In my feeble attempt to justify the move, I explained the difference in tuition costs.

"Are we poor?" you wanted to know.

"No, we're not poor," I said. I stumbled into another explanation because you knew your dad and I had good salaries and saved for your tuition and school expenses. "We will be able to take better vacations, golf vacations, because of the money we'd save on the lower tuition at UDJ."

That response seemed to satisfy you. Still for the first few months you continued to complain every day when you came home from school. Bran, you loathed attending an all-boy school. At Country

Day, you were the resident heartthrob and the must-have guest at every kid's birthday party. When classmates invited you to parties, their mothers called me if I didn't RSVP in a timely manner.

"Brandon is coming, isn't he?" they would ask. "We can't have a party without Brandon!"

When we decided to transfer you, I can't tell you how many mothers asked me, "Why are you taking Brandon away from us?"

What we didn't tell you, Bran, was that we felt you had been the victim of some racist attitudes at Country Day that you weren't even aware of, and we felt it was necessary to increase your awareness of what being a young black man in America entails.

As much as changing schools was a considerable adjustment for you, that initial resistance was short-lived. Your charismatic personality quickly gained you a new circle of friends. And you came to see the benefits of this change in your life.

Yes, Brandon, you certainly settled in. Your personality remained robust, and you were soon known as the smart boy who talked too much. It was challenging and sometimes exhausting for me, as I found myself tactfully figuring out how to curtail your behavior in school without diminishing that distinctive attribute I loved about you. I soon discovered this worry was unwarranted.

I believe this occurred in one of your eighth-grade classes at UDJ. Apparently, Bran, as you told the story, your teacher thought he would punish and embarrass you for talking in class by having you stand on a desk and sing "I'm a Little Teapot."

Later at home, you joyfully told me, "Mom, I sang the best version of 'I'm a Little Teapot' they had ever heard!" You continued by demonstrating how you kept singing it over and over until the teacher finally said, "Okay, Brandon, that's enough."

I don't remember if you received a detention for that performance, but as we both know, you received your share of detentions at UDJ. (The boys called detentions JUGS, for Judgment Under God.) Some of them may have been for tardiness, which I must take responsibility for during the years I was driving you to school. But of course, your outspokenness was mostly the culprit.

Do you remember our talk about having you take responsibility for your actions? Well, I do. You thought some of your detentions were given unfairly. Brandon, I advised you to speak with your teachers in private about that, which you did on several occasions. You prided yourself in convincing a teacher that you didn't deserve a particular JUG, and you delighted in telling me so. You didn't know this, Bran, but you were honing your negotiation skills.

In my effort to keep you safe, I taught you to be especially mindful when you were in the suburbs with your Caucasian friends because if there were any type of disturbance, you were likely to be singled out. After you started driving, I repeatedly spoke these words, "If you are stopped by a police officer, place your hands in plain view. Speak slowly and politely. Say 'Yes, sir' or 'No, sir' and 'Yes, ma'am' or 'No, ma'am,' as appropriate. Do all the talking and insist that everyone else in the vehicle remain silent." So to anyone who asks if our young black sons are raised differently, I would reply, "They had better be!"

By the time you reached ninth grade, you were feeling confident and accomplished about yourself as a student and UDJ Cub. Your grades were excellent while in the academy, and by now you knew your way around school, compared to all the newly entering ninth-graders who didn't have two years of UDJ behind them.

As a high school freshman, you made the Cubs junior varsity golf team. Your teammates said you impressed them on the first day of golf tryouts. Other freshmen were nervous and intimidated, but not you. In my opinion, you were a little too high on yourself. It seemed that good times and golf were your main focus as you entered your freshman year.

I painfully recall attending a parent-teacher conference during which I was stunned to hear other than the usual glowing accounts of your academic success. I was accustomed to the behavior-related concerns like "Brandon talks in class" or "Mrs. Spight, please encourage Brandon to pursue a career in speaking because he never stops." Instead I was confronted with, "I know Brandon is bright, but he's not turning in his assignments" or "Brandon didn't do well on the last test."

One teacher commented that you perhaps were feeling a little cocky, figuring you were a UDJ veteran after two years in the academy compared to other ninth-graders who were newbies to the school's rigor. She said that was an unfortunate but common ninth-grade/high school bug that sometimes bites. It had certainly bitten you.

Teacher after teacher related the same scenario. After providing me with a disappointing academic report, more than one of them said, "But I hear he's a great golfer!" By the time I returned home, I was livid. I could barely control my anger as I waited for you and your dad to return from—where else?—the golf course!

When you returned home, I gave you both a piece of my mind. I recounted what each teacher had said to me, and I told you how upset I was that the only good news I heard was praise for your golf game. Really?! I had no appreciation for your golf talent at that moment. As you expected, a punishment was in your future.

Bran, we both know that over the course of your upbringing, I was the main disciplinarian. You were no stranger to losing privileges at home. Your teachers, starting as early as Country Day, would inform me of behavior issues, "Brandon is bright, but he doesn't raise his hand before responding," "Brandon finishes his work and then wants to talk to his neighbor," or "Brandon likes to entertain his classmates." I would explain to your teachers that our family gatherings were loud and demonstrative, filled with relatives who relished taking center stage and providing stories and jokes resulting in hearty laughter. Let's face it: the main characters were your dad and your Uncle Clyde! So I would tell your teachers that, unfortunately, school was your stage and your classmates were your audience. As anticipated, your teachers were not amused. That feeble attempt was for you, Bran. I would then end the discussion with a conciliatory, "I'll talk to Brandon."

Even though I completely understood the origin of your personality, you and I would discuss the appropriate behavior I expected from you. Remember the contracts I had you sign? These contracts were in keeping with my persistent attempts to raise a responsible and respectful young man.

There was the contract of May 4, 1998, stipulating your responsibilities regarding the care of our newly acquired, six-week-old kitten, Haley. Haley was the compromise pet negotiated by me when you, Bran, really wanted a dog.

Your responsibilities included cleaning the kitty litter box every evening, brushing her hair every other day, and feeding her "at the direction and/or supervision of Constance J. Spight. Any violation of the below terms gives Constance J. Spight every right to terminate food, shelter, and care for said kitten/cat." You also signed a contract on February 5, 2002, promising "never to argue with my mom about doing my homework."

Of course, there were some lapses, which required me to refer you back to the contract. You were pretty reliable, however, but sometimes tardy about cleaning the litter box. Homework, on the other hand, continued to be a challenge despite the contract.

So after suffering through that disappointing parent-teacher conference, I had no choice but to reinstill once again the importance of your responsibilities.

As a punishment was pondered, I knew your dad would rebuke my efforts to take away your golf privileges. So among the ways I sought to punish you were to take away your phone, ban video games and TV, or ground you from activities with your friends.

When you were younger and we took away your privileges, your worst punishments were when you were confined to your room. You would be allowed to write, draw, or read but not be allowed to play video games or watch your TV. Once you said to me, "It's okay, Mom. I like to read."

What you didn't like was the separation from what was going on in other parts of the house. If the doorbell rang, you would call out, "Who's at the door, Mom?"

As a teenager though, confining you to your room seemed juvenile. I decided that TV elimination was more appropriate, but that proved to be impossible when your dad was home. You managed to get around this punishment by joining your dad in the family room, where he would have the TV on. There you would sit attentively watching something we all knew you had no personal interest in.

"Did you forget, Virgil, that Brandon was on punishment?" I'd ask your dad.

Virgil's reply was, "I'm not on punishment."

I would also resort to taking away your phone and restricting you from after-school fun by demanding that you come straight home from school to do homework. You subverted that, however, by having fun visit you. You were supposed to be on lockdown when one of your closest buddies, Richerd Winton, came over after school one day. When I got home, the two of you were in the family room.

"You're on punishment. Why is Richerd here?" I asked.

You said you didn't interpret that to mean Richerd couldn't come over after school. That rationale wasn't at all surprising since Richerd spent so much time at our house, we thought he was moving in!

"That means you're both on punishment now," said your dad.

But no matter the contract or my expectations for your behavior, your dad remained steadfast, preventing me from eliminating golf as a punishment.

"I didn't want him to have negative feelings about the game," explained your dad. He had grand plans for your golf future, perhaps as a pro player. "Whatever I could do to help and motivate him, I wanted to do it. Besides, it wasn't golf for pleasure. It was golf practice. That's more like work!"

Speaking of work, at the age of sixteen, I believed you were old enough for a part-time job, so one day I told you to go job-hunting after school. Your dad wasn't in favor, but I convinced him this was to instill responsibility. You came home telling me how impressed the mall store managers were when they saw you and your friends in your school shirts and ties.

"You and your friends?" I questioned.

"Yes, Mom, my friends wanted to go too."

As I was finishing my lecture as to why you don't go apply for jobs with your friends, your dad chimed in, "Bran, I'll give you a job."

We both turned to your dad, anxiously waiting to hear the offer. He continued, "If you practice golf four days a week for two hours each day, I'll pay you."

Bran, you didn't see me grimace at your dad. You were too consumed with thoughts of negotiating a higher salary. I don't recall the amount your dad offered, but when he walked away, you turned to me and said, "Mom, I think I should negotiate a better deal."

"Seriously, Brandon?" I responded. "You need to take this deal, or you'll be pounding the pavement again tomorrow job hunting … alone!"

I never took away your driver's license, but I delayed you getting it when your GPA fell to a C average.

"Mom, it's a C-plus! And I'm at U of D. At any other school, it would be a B-plus!" is how you explained it.

"Look, Brandon, you know you can do better," I told you. "And you're not getting your driver's license until you bring up your GPA."

Once again, you were angry at your mom. But that was okay. You knew you weren't doing your best. By the next card marking, you were a solid B.

I drew up your driving contract on June 9, 2006. You signed it with the following terms and restrictions:

You will provide destination and time of return.

You will drive directly home from school unless prior advisement to parents has occurred.

Your seat belt as well as each passenger's in the vehicle will be worn.

You will drive with no more than three passengers.

You will not drive while eating or talking on your cell phone.

You will not drive if you become impaired in any way— You will immediately call your parents at that point.

You will not allow anyone else to drive your vehicle.

You will always drive at a safe speed.

If stopped by the police, you will display hands at all times, remain calm, and be polite. Should you feel that treatment was unjust, make note of officer's name and badge number to provide to parents.

You will arrive home no later than twelve midnight, unless permission to exceed is obtained. This restriction may be modified in the future.

Bran, you did well adhering to the terms of the driving contract. We were especially pleased and proud about how you explained your interaction when you were stopped by police in Dearborn, a suburb notorious for its history of racist attitudes against African Americans.

"Mom, I was stopped by the Dearborn police today," you told me after you had gone to see your friend Teleicia Rose play in a school golf match in the area.

My stomach tightened, and my heart started beating faster. "So what happened, Bran?"

"He stopped me. I made sure he could see my hands on the wheel, Mom. He asked me for my license and registration and told me I was speeding."

The officer asked more questions about why you were in the area. You were still wearing your tie and dress shirt from school, and you explained that you had been to a golf tournament to see your friend play.

"A girl?" the officer asked.

"Yes," you replied.

Then the officer asked which school you attended, and you told him University of Detroit Jesuit.

"Well, young man, I'm going to give you a warning today. You need to slow down," he told you, handed back your license and registration, and sent you on your way home.

"So you didn't tell him your parents were on the Detroit police force?" I asked him.

"No, Mom, I didn't need to," you said. "I had him at U of D."

Marty LaRouere, "Big Fella," recounts,

Brandon: Always Loved and Never Forgotten

I am so proud and honored to say that Brandon was my first friend at U of D Jesuit, a place I hold very close to my heart. U of D taught and prepared me to live a life with integrity, passion, intellectual curiosity, and an awareness for my fellow man. Brandon was the first student at U of D who introduced me to these important concepts and helped me adjust to life as a U of D Cub.

I first met Brandon at the place he loved the most, a golf course. It was at golf tryouts in August where all the freshmen were nervous and apprehensive about playing and meeting new people, but not Brandon. I vividly remember him talking, joking, and talking some more that morning. I thought to myself, "How can someone be so full of energy at 6:15 a.m.?" But little did I know, that was the kind of person Brandon was.

Walking the courses of Palmer Park, Rackham, and Detroit Golf Club with Brandon are some of my fondest memories. While some people may think golf is a very dull or unexciting game, Brandon made sure that wasn't true when he played.

I can recall times when he shouted in support of a teammate a few holes behind him, called a penalty on an opposing school in a very blunt and humorous way, or smashed a 300-yard drive and made sure everyone on the course knew he did so.

I always enjoyed arguing with him. Somehow Brandon always found a way to make a valid point, forcing me to agree with him or quickly change the subject. I always knew Brandon would have made the perfect litigation lawyer.

One of our most memorable arguments was about who was the greatest golfer in the world: Vijay Singh or Tiger Woods. I took Vijay's side; Brandon took Tiger's. I didn't back down for years. But in light of Tiger's miraculous US Open victory in June 2008 despite his knee injury, I will again take Brandon's side. And I'm sure he was there to cheer on his golf idol every step of the way that weekend.

Golf connected Brandon and me. And the connection I made with him represented a more important connection that Brandon was responsible for. U of D is a very diverse school. I felt that Brandon was the bridge between different races at U of D. He was such a likable person, and his enthusiasm rubbed off on others. No matter a person's racial background, Brandon was able to interact with him or her. Because of this unique and admirable ability, I believe Brandon was the prime, firsthand example of making judgments based on a person's character rather than on their appearance.

And speaking of appearance, Brandon made sure he always looked good. He would craft a flawless outfit, whether at school, playing golf, or an event on the weekend. There are many times I remember him ironing his golf shirts before a 7:00 a.m. round, protecting his Jordan shoes, having the perfect necktie knot, or sporting the occasional pink golf shirt on the course. His flashy smile, clean clothes, shiny hole-in-one necklace, and beaming personality spoke for themselves.

And one of his attributes that cannot go unnoticed was his sense of humor. Brandon stories would constantly circulate around the school, especially among the golf team. I thoroughly enjoyed hearing Brandon's account of his latest JUG (Judgment Under God, a detention), his argument with a teacher over a letter grade, or how he met a fine-looking girl at the latest dance.

From smashing tacos on a friend's car to blaring music in a parking lot, antagonizing kids from Brother Rice and St. Mary's, proclaiming Serena Williams his future wife, his inherent fear of bees, and giving me the nickname "Big Fella," I have stories that I can laugh about and tell to others for the rest of my life.

And that brings me to the reason I chose to write about Brandon in this journalistic style of writing. Journalism is based on being able to write about and convey a story. Brandon's life is remembered by so many interesting, admirable, and certainly entertaining stories. I feel privileged and forever grateful that I can be one of the many storytellers of Brandon Spight.

Bran, we often convey how you made a statement on the golf course, but Teleicia Rose has a different perspective.

Thinking back on all the times, laughs, and tears that Brandon and I shared, I believe one of my fondest memories was our first "date." Brandon was my date for my senior-year award ceremony. We were clearly the two best-dressed people at the entire event, but that's neither here nor there.

The night went smoothly until it was time to leave. There had been multiple altercations throughout the night, and they had escalated into threats of physical violence. As we were walking toward the car, shouts rang out that there was a man with a gun, and the crowd began to scatter. But not Brandon! He was too cool to crease his loafers or wrinkle his finely tailored suit. (That's "B" for you; even in the face of danger, he must stay fly!) I sprinted toward the car, assuming Brandon was behind me. I turned around, and he was slowly strolling across the parking lot. He even had the audacity to pause and flip his coattails!

Needless to say, he got an earful from me the entire ride home. I turned to him and yelled, "Who do you think you are, Superman?" His calm reply was a nonchalant "Yes."

After that, he always made it a point to joke about his run-in with a "gunman on 15 Mile" and how he'd never visit again because the suburbs were too "hood." Since that day, he's been my Superman: fearless in the face of danger, calm under pressure, quick to react,

dependable (regardless of the time), my rock, my friend, invincible …
simply put, my Superman.

I love you, Brandon. Always have and always will.

Teleicia Rose

Yes, Brandon, you certainly had a flair. Because I hated to iron, I taught you how to iron your shirts and jeans. So as Marty said, it was not uncommon for you to iron your golf shirt before a 7:00 a.m. tee time. Remember your red golf shirt that you absolutely loved? And how when your dad accidentally bleached it in the wash, you were livid? But you wore the shirt anyway.

"Why are you wearing it?" I questioned.

You said, "I'm protesting Dad messing up my shirt!"

I wish I could recall how you played that day!

And as everyone knows by now, you coined the phrase "Real men wear pink!" because you often sported the electric pink polo shirt or sweater on the golf course. You told me it was in honor of my Alpha Kappa Alpha sorority colors, pink and green. Well, Bran, that's another fashion statement you made that appears to have prompted change because it's not unusual to see a golfer in a pink shirt these days.

You were not naïve to the attitudes of other golf teams. I distinctly remember you telling me that when your team played other schools, as you waited in the clubhouse to prepare for the tournament, you often sported your earplugs as you listened to your iPod.

At one event, an opposing team player attempted to taunt you, "Why are you here playing golf instead of somewhere rapping?"

You took out your earplugs and asked, "What did you say?" You took great pleasure in showing that guy exactly why you were there that day.

I think you felt you had something to prove. African Americans are rare in professional golf, despite the success of legends such as Calvin Peete and Tiger Woods. African Americans certainly were rare in the Detroit-area Catholic high school golf leagues. Besides your teammate Mark, there were no other African-American young men playing golf in the Detroit Catholic High School League. You told us about other times when you experienced outward hostility from other teams, but you took all this in stride because you knew you were different. You had known it for a long time.

Even before you joined the UDJ team, people watched you intensely on the golf course. Other golfers walked up to ask your name and wrote it down, as if they wanted to remember when and where they first saw you.

"I want to remember you," one gentleman said, "because I'm going to see you on the pro circuit one day."

They could see it in your swing, demeanor, and comfort on the course. Maybe they could even see in your eyes that you were going to play professional golf one day. And the more people who watched you, the larger your gallery, the better you seemed to play. Even though you played for an all-boy school, sometimes your female friends came to watch you play.

While you excelled as a golfer, you also shined as a teammate. That's what your UDJ coach, Paul Diehl, told us. A golfer can easily forget about the team to concentrate on individual success. "You can be a great golfer and not be a good teammate," Coach said. "But there wasn't a better guy as a teammate on or off the golf course than Brandon."

Yes, it was your nature to shout encouragement to a teammate playing behind you. But it was also your nature to point out a penalty on an opposing school's player in a very loud and humorous but determined way or smash one of your trademark 300-yard drives and make sure everybody on the other team knew about it!

Nick Hammer, your friend since the seventh grade and probably your closest friend on the golf team, remembers a day of your senior year when UDJ beat its big rival, Warren De La Salle, by seven strokes. "We were all in their parking lot, dancing away, singing the school song at the top of our lungs, just being kids," Nick says.

The De La Salle team was giving the Cubs the evil eye, but Nick says you kept dancing, Bran, celebrating and singing louder than before. Perhaps it wasn't your most sportsmanlike moment, but I'm guessing you were caught up in the excitement and so very proud of the team's win.

As much as you were encouraging on the golf course, when you played with your friends in a casual setting, you weren't above talking trash about how someone was playing. Charlie Johnson, who was not on the golf team, remembers a particular occasion.

"I was having a particularly horrid round," Charlie recounts. He remembers seeing you walk toward him and feeling a sense of calm as he was expecting your usual words of support as well as a pep talk. Instead, Bran, you looked at his scorecard and taunted, "Charlie, you suck!"

Bran, when Charlie told this story, we all laughed, including Charlie. Charlie has this uncanny ability to imitate your voice!

You were a team player, even when you did not play. In the golf regionals your senior year, you were the odd man out. Five U of D golfers were going to regionals, and you were the sixth man.

"When he got the news, there was no, 'You're crazy. I'm the best player. You should pick me instead,'" Coach Diehl remembers. "It was really a professional response. I was kind of surprised, to be honest, that someone that young could handle it so well."

You know, Bran, as your mom, I recall your profound disappointment on that occasion. But it fueled your desire to improve and move on to the next challenge. You focused on playing golf in college.

Coach Diehl wrote the following as a tribute to you:

Dear Brandon,

It's Mr. Diehl, your golf coach. This letter is to give testimony to how much your life continues to work wonders, even though you no longer are physically with us. The force of your personality, determination, and accomplishments continue to impact your fellow students, teammates, coaches, friends, and family.

Let's go over the facts. The University of Detroit Jesuit High golf program had its most successful season in decades in 2008. The junior varsity maroon team won the Catholic League regular season as well as the championship tournament. The JV white team, composed mainly of freshmen, went undefeated in nine-hole play.

Your varsity teammates won the Catholic League Central Division title for the first time since 1981! The team went 7-1, with a dramatic one-stroke victory over Brother Rice at Oakland Hills in its final match to clinch the title. The team won two ties with a fifth-man tiebreaker. The varsity won its regional tournament for the first time since 2003! At state finals, the Cubs finished in the top ten in Division 1. Wow!

What contributed to these great accomplishments? My imagination reminds me of the movie Angels in the Outfield, in which baseball-loving angels manipulated hits from the heavens. Do I think you, Brandon, are directing golf balls into the cups for U-D High? I'll admit it has crossed my mind. But what I am sure of is that you have given us something intangible this season. It's the legacy of your special spirit.

I talked to the players last summer at our golf trip. I told them that they had to work as hard as I know you would have. I also talked about your commitment to the team. No one wanted to play in state finals more than you. Unfortunately you never got that chance. You showed class and poise when you were denied the opportunity, but you still craved that chance.

You always were a team player. You were part of our celebration against De La Salle early in your senior year. Everyone was excited over that seven-stroke victory. The team sang the fight song in the parking lot in the dark that night while you whooped it up. You could be counted on for various antics on the team golf trip in August. It wasn't until this year that the team told me about a hole in a wall that Coach DiMambro was able to help take care of after a sock fight that you hosted.

I felt you let each Cub golfer know that they could accomplish great things if they worked hard and had faith in themselves and the team. The state regional qualifier is the best example of your touch at work. I usually am a wreck that day. It is the hardest and most important day of the year for the team. This year I never worried. No player had a bad day. They finished strong, and we won by one stroke over De La Salle.

The program wants to thank you for your effort and spirit. We have an award for you at school. It reads, "This annual award is bestowed upon the senior golfer, voted by his teammates, who best exemplifies the qualities of Brandon: Sportsmanship, Charisma, Leadership, and Dedication."

Ronnie Young was selected by his teammates to win the award in 2008. He's a great kid. He worked very hard. He finished fourth out of 264 players in one tournament. He won All-Catholic honors at the Catholic League Championship. Ronnie used to be happy just to make the team. This year, Ronnie played in state finals at Grand Valley State University!

Brandon Spight, thanks for all your gifts to us.

From Coach Diehl

When we began looking at colleges for you, I felt it was time for you to be an active participant in the selection process. After all, you were seventeen, and it would be where you'd spend the next four years of your life. Our prior educational placement decisions for you were based on your dad and I wanting you to be in the best academic position for the next phase of your education, and I believe we accomplished that goal. So it was your turn to customize your own higher education and find the right college fit. Surprisingly you had no demands as to which college you would attend.

You said your only requirement was a school where "I can play golf all year round," so those were the institutions I began sending your way to consider. Among them were Eastern Michigan University (your dad's suggestion), Hampton University, Bethune-Cookman University, Johnson C. Smith University, and Morehouse College. Sometimes you would turn to me with a puzzled expression and say, "Mom, I never even heard of this school!" In general though, you kept an open mind.

Personally, I wanted you to be a Morehouse man. You initially howled at the idea of attending another all-male school, until it was pointed out that the private, all-female Spelman College was a stone's throw away! I was further encouraged by a conversation your dad had with a gentleman (connected to Morehouse) he played golf with who was impressed with your dad's golf game.

Your dad told him, "Well, my son is a better golfer than me." At which point the man asked Virgil to keep him informed of your college-bound status. You were still alive when your acceptance letter from Eastern Michigan University arrived. Your dad was thrilled, but you weren't impressed. Unfortunately, Bran, you were gone when the other acceptance letters arrived. Every school accepted you, and I cried while reading each letter.

Bran, as you know, you embarked on a series of campus tours to explore potential colleges. As it happened, a new line of Air Jordans was being released on the same day as one of your trips. You gave me money and begged me to buy a pair for you. I reluctantly went to the store early and stood in line, all the while fielding constant calls from you to update my status.

"Where are you in the line, Mom? How many pairs do you think they have left?" You were a little obsessive, to say the least!

A girl standing behind me in line, after overhearing our conversation, told me her mother would never go through such an ordeal for her. That made me feel good, but I assured her I was only there because you were on a college tour.

Coach Diehl wrote a letter of recommendation for you. He wrote,

> *Brandon is a hard worker, who never stops trying to improve his swing and his score. He focuses as much energy as he can on being a good player. He is a good team player. I have never had to discipline Brandon in all the time we were together. He wants what is best for the team. Brandon has spent a great deal of time in summer tournaments. His play improved thanks to his participation on the PowerBilt Tour. He has improved his overall game, in large measure due to his dedication and perseverance. His combined average of nine-hole and eighteen-hole competition was 79.14. Brandon has great family support. His parents are dedicated to seeing him get a great education as well as an opportunity to play college golf.*

But it was left to you to convey to college admission officials how your pursuit of excellence in competitive golf shaped your character and your goals.

That you did, even as you struggled with headaches and an unknown adversary within your own body. You finished your college essay in between doctor's appointments, diagnostic scans, and semester exams, just days before you were admitted to the hospital. Even with pain sapping your strength, you remained focused on telling your story.

BRANDON'S PERSONAL STATEMENT FOR HIS COLLEGE ESSAY

When I made my decision to become proficient in the game of golf, I didn't realize it would require me to live as a chameleon. I am not fickle; however, I am the type of person who can adapt to situations that would cause discomfort to most. I am an African American who grew up experiencing two extremes my entire life. As a three-year-old, I would wake up every morning at six o'clock to get ready for school. After getting dressed and eating breakfast, one of my parents would drive me to one of the best schools in the state of Michigan, Detroit Country Day. My parents made a sacrifice every day to drive forty-five minutes from the city of Detroit to the suburbs to ensure I received the best education possible. Even at the tender age of three, I realized I was one of three African Americans in the lower school. Surprisingly being in such a small minority did not bother me at all. As an outgoing and self-assured person, making friends in all races and becoming popular was easy for me. I had such a good time learning and making friends that I was blind to unjust treatment I received. However, as I matured and recalled certain events, this type of treatment became very apparent.

Additionally, and much to my surprise, the African Americans in my neighborhood and even some family members treated me differently because of the school I attended and because I chose to learn golf instead of basketball or football. Those closest to me seemed not to respect me because I did not play the traditional sports normally played by African Americans. Subsequently, as a way to be accepted and make friends in the neighborhood, I started playing basketball.

When I would meet new people, I would tell them I played basketball and not mention golf. In my neighborhood, golf wasn't a sport I was supposed to play. I was labeled as a stuck-up black boy trying to be white. It got to the point where I had to use the slang of the neighborhood kids when I was home in order to be accepted. When I went to school, I would modify my speech and behavior to be accepted in that environment. Perfecting that skill has created lasting friendships in both worlds. One might say this is phony behavior; however, I feel it is adaptability.

The older I became, I realized the sport I loved was golf. I have played this game since the age of three despite enduring racist attitudes. These attitudes continue to be apparent when I walk through the golf course parking lot or step onto the first tee. The looks that people give me when I swing the club could burn a hole through a wall. However, after I hit a good shot, the look of astonishment is far more satisfying. I have learned to play through the looks, attitudes, and racist comments. I gained respect by posting good scores.

As I look back on my experiences I had growing up, I actually feel extremely fortunate. I may have gone through some struggles, but they ended up making me a stronger and well-rounded person. Today, I take pride in the fact that I not only play golf, but I am very good at it. Despite all the mockery I received growing up, I was able to move past that and continue doing what I love. The only thing I can hope for is that maybe I changed a person's view on stereotyping African Americans in sports. Hopefully they looked at me and realized you don't have to do something because a majority does it. A person is supposed to pursue his passion and do what makes him happy despite what people think, which is how I have lived my life up to this point and will continue to do so for the rest of my life.

Brandon Lee Spight

6

DAYS OF ANGUISH AND ACCEPTANCE

A few days after you were admitted to Beaumont Hospital, Bran, your dad and I believed we were witnessing a miracle. You started to look better and act livelier. Even our neurosurgeon was pleased, commenting that you were a strong young man. It was as if you were going to defeat this horrible monster in your brain after all. I had renewed optimism and felt like our prayers were being answered.

I maintained my sanity by convincing myself that you would be fine. My focus was on how our lives would change during your recovery. I mentally made plans to suspend my real estate business so I could concentrate on your rehabilitation therapy and arrangements with your school to complete your senior year. I knew it would be important to you to graduate with your 2007 classmates.

When our dear friend, Cleophus "Buzzy" Boyd, came to see you one day, you were unusually welcoming and even talked briefly. Buzzy was accustomed to playing golf with you. He was part of the Sunday golfing group that your dad made you a part of as well. On the occasion your dad didn't golf because he had a fishing tournament, Buzzy would call to see if you could play. I teased him on occasion about a grown man asking, "Can Brandon come out to play?" But I realized then, and even more so now, that this was a testament to you, Bran, and your relationship with him and the other golfers.

As he was about to leave the hospital, Buzzy told you that being in the hospital was no excuse for playing golf badly. The next time you and he met on the course, Buzzy said, he vowed to show you no mercy, even though he had beaten you only once before.

You looked at him, and through your pain and sedation, the Brandon we knew shined through. You smiled. "Ain't no way," you responded. It was an encouraging moment.

Buzzy's written reflection embraces his most memorable golf outings with you.

It seems so funny, after living more than fifteen years in Lansing, Michigan, and acquiring many personal reminiscences, the memories that stick out most in my mind are those of returning with Brandon, his dad, Virgil, and my daughter, Keli, for our July weekend of golf tournaments at MSU's Forest Akers golf courses. The first tournament would be the local Dick Letts Memorial on Saturday, followed by the outing of our club, the Sunday Headsmen, on Sunday.

Brandon would always say in preparation for this trip, "Hey, Buzzy, we're going to Happy Lansing," as though he were Dorothy from The Wizard of Oz, speaking of Kansas. Although Keli didn't play golf, she always wanted to drive the golf cart. And on more than one occasion, Virgil would catch Brandon straying from the seriousness of our competition, sitting on the cart with Keli playing Game Boy videos. They were friends. And for as long as I can remember, at least according to Virgil and me, they were going to one day get married to each other. I'm sure at the very mention of that scenario they would simply laugh and indulge us our "proud Poppa" moment. After golf, Keli and Brandon usually would go swimming at the University Club, and from there, after eating, we would find our way over to Maggie Moo's ice cream parlor in the Town Center Mall. It was a weekend trip to which we all looked forward. And although I and Keli have made the trip again, it wasn't the same without Brandon: Neither Forest Akers, Maggie Moo's, or Happy Lansing.

Many times when I am listening to Keli talk or watching her dance to and repeat every word of a rap video, I think of Brandon. They both knew all the words to the latest T.I. flow or old-school Temptations. "Musically and culturally diverse" is how I categorized them, keeping up with their generation's hard-core musical tastes while appreciating and enjoying their parents' songs of love and happiness. I can still see them with their headphones and iPods, rapping and bopping to the beat together.

Even today when I hear Keli speak, I hear Brandon. Her cadence and mannerisms are much like his. Or perhaps she is simply a reflection of what made me, Janice, Virgil, and Connie so proud of our late-in-life kids. Confident, creative, sensitive, smart, with clarity of vision and purpose: all the things that made, and make, the sacrifices—and yes, even the heartache and tears—valuable events. I remember the last time I spoke to Brandon. He was showing remarkable progress after being admitted a day or so earlier into Beaumont Hospital. Through the haze and medication, he recognized me. We made small talk. And finally, just as I was about to leave, I told him that his being in the hospital was not going to be an acceptable excuse for a poor golf game. The next time we played together, there would be no mercy. I was going to (as I had done only once before) beat him. He looked at me and, with unmistakable confidence, said, "Ain't no way." Little did I know then, for all the wrong reasons, he was right.

Still missing you,

Cleophus "Buzzy" Boyd

One night our neurosurgeon stopped by to see you in your

hospital room. I thought, *How dedicated he is to come see you so late.* But then I worried there might be a problem. Had he seen something in your tests that concerned him?

No, he said he was there to deliver some bad news to a couple about their baby: their child was brain dead. *How awful,* I thought. We instinctively felt concern for the parents faced with such dreadful news. Not once, however, did I think that your dad and I would also be those parents one day.

Unfortunately the optimism we had faded day by day. And watching you struggle, in body and in spirit, was heartbreaking. I'll never forget the turmoil you were in one night in the hospital. Your words ripped through my heart that night. Sadly that memory still has a way of tearing me down today. You were terribly distraught. You kept asking me why God had not made you well.

"Why is God mad at me?" you pleaded with me. "What have I done?"

As I looked into your troubled, frenzied eyes, I struggled to find words of encouragement. "God is not mad at you, Bran. You haven't done anything wrong. I don't know why you're not better yet. You're alive. You're going to get better. Please try to calm down."

My attempt to console you was futile. You kept asking, "What did I do? Please, God, if I've done something wrong, I'm sorry! I'll never do it again! Please, God, let me get better!"

The pain and anguish I heard from your lips, I felt deep in my soul. That night, I sat with you until you fell asleep. Then I went out into the hallway because I could no longer control myself as I cried and pleaded with God. I found myself sliding down the wall and landing on the floor. I don't know how long I sat there. I must have triggered the automatic doors, but I was oblivious to their repeated opening and closing until I heard someone say, "Please step away from the doors."

I crawled away until I was no longer activating the sensor.

Eventually I returned to your room and just sat watching you sleep. I whispered, "Please, God, hear my son."

That was a very long night. Those memories are forever stamped into the crevices of my brain. I felt so incredibly useless. I couldn't answer your question, Bran, because I was asking God the same. It was remarkable to me the number of people, some of them complete strangers, who would tell me to pray. "Ask God to heal him," they would whisper. Or more amazing still, others would ask, "Are you praying?"

I would just stare at them! *Am I praying? What do you think I'm doing? What else can I do?* I wanted to scream out, "This is my child! Of course I'm praying!"

The bleed in your brain appeared to be worsening. Outwardly, you exhibited anger and frustration, but I think inwardly you were mostly afraid. You tired of the repetitive questions from the hospital staff: "What is your name? How old are you? Where are you? What year is it?" At one point, you refused to respond. Your dad had a conversation with you in private, and after that you responded to the questions. However, there were days you wouldn't talk. Whether it was the result of the bleed, the medication, or depression, I'm not sure. I believe your silence with visitors had more to do with embarrassment over your condition.

When your UDJ golf teammate Mark DiMambro called and asked if he could come to visit, I allowed him to come but forewarned him that you might not speak. He wanted to come regardless. Mark stood by your bed and spoke to you nonstop about school, golf, and your friendship, and you never let your gaze drop as you looked at him without saying a word. The nonverbal Brandon was unknown to Mark, but it did not deter his words or his concern for you.

The best memory I have of Brandon happened on a bright fall day at the Detroit Golf Club in a match during the season. Brandon had teed off in the group before me and had been struggling on the first few holes.

He was one or two over after three holes, and while I was on the third hole, I happened to peer over to the fourth tee box. Brandon was hitting a shot from about twenty yards behind the tee. I had no idea what was going on or why he would do that, but I learned he had hit his drive against a tree and the ball had deflected off it. It actually went behind the tee box. He had hit a drive minus twenty yards! After already starting the day off on a bad foot and seeing that mishap, I wrote Brandon down for a score in the mid to high forties.

Later I finished my round and went up to Brandon, who appeared very irked. I was preparing myself for a huuuge number. I went up and asked him how the day went, and he told me he had shot even par thirty-four. I had to stop and think for a second. Then I asked him again what he had shot. He emphatically replied again, "Thirty-four."

Little did I know that Brandon finished the fourth hole with a seven and then went on to go birdie, eagle, par, birdie, and par to finish the day at even par.

To this day, I have never been more astonished by an accomplishment of a personal friend. To come back and finish that strong shows the tremendous character that Brandon possessed. He could have mailed in the round, but he stuck with it and was the main reason we ended up winning our match that day.

It was an honor getting to know Brandon for those four years, and his positivity and integrity rubbed off on everyone around him. He was never scared to stand up for what he believed in, and I admired the heck out of him for that. He didn't shy away from confrontation because he knew that if he had to be confrontational to make things right, then it was the right thing to do.

I will never forget the smile he brought not only to my face, but also to the faces of all the students at The High every day he was around.

Mark DiMambro

I slept at your bedside every night, and your dad was there very late into the evenings too. I never wanted to leave the hospital, but your dad insisted, so when he returned in the morning, I would go home to shower and change clothes, but mostly I spent that time hysterically crying in private so I could appear calm when I returned to the hospital. Rarely would your dad and I take a break at the same time, but if we did, usually your Auntie Cheryl, my best friend since high school and your second mom, took our place. Somebody was always visiting you, sitting with you, or praying for you.

On Thursday, February 8, when I returned to your hospital room from a run home to shower, I could instantly see that something was not right with you. "What's going on?" I asked your dad.

"What do you mean?"

"Something is wrong with Brandon." Your left arm was awkwardly angled across your chest. "Are you okay?" I asked.

You said, "Yes."

"Are you in pain?"

"No," but I sensed you had suffered another brain bleed because your gaze was vacant.

I urgently called for the nurse. I blamed myself for going home to shower, convinced that this bleed would not have occurred had I been there. I was your savior. No one else could help you but me, I thought, obviously the thoughts of a deranged mom losing control of her faculties because I was losing you.

I asked if you were hungry, and you answered yes, so I tried to feed you from the tray placed by your bed. You were sitting partially upright in your bed.

"Chew your food, Bran," I said.

You whispered, "I am."

But as I fed you, you just held the food in your mouth. Without hesitation, I removed the food from your mouth with my fingers. I feared you would choke, concluding that your damaged brain was not able to tell you to chew. By then the nurse had returned to tell me she had called the doctor.

But you, Bran, wanted to tell me something. Without saying a word, you raised your right hand and grabbed mine. To my astonishment, you started twisting my hand in a very familiar fashion. You were trying to do our own personal, goofy handshake!

Sometimes you used to call me "Home Slice," and you invented this cute handshake to go with it. I don't know where the nickname or handshake came from. But every time you left home, you would say, "Okay, Home Slice, I'm out" and do your little handshake routine with me, and we would snap our fingers at the end. As you raced out the door, I always yelled after you, "Be careful!"

Well, at the hospital that evening, I was excited when you insisted on doing the Home Slice handshake with me! You kept doing it over and over and over again. You even snapped your fingers!

I asked, "Are we doing our handshake?"

You didn't respond. You just kept staring into my eyes and doing our handshake. Except for your right arm, I realized that the rest of your body seemed to have stiffened. When I asked you to move your left arm, it didn't move. I asked again if you were in pain, and you said no. Still, you did not take your eyes off me.

Your dad and your granddad were in the room with me. Your dad was at the foot of your bed, and I asked, "Who is this?"

"Dad," you replied without looking at your dad, not taking your eyes off me.

Your granddad was on the opposite and left side of your bed. "And who is this?" I asked.

You hesitated, and I realized it was because you couldn't turn your head to see. "The doctor?" you guessed.

I immediately regretted asking the question. Your grandfather was visibly shaken, Bran. In that moment, his heart broke. He stood there wiping away tears and left the hospital shortly afterward. That was the last time your granddad came to the hospital. It was the last time he would see you alive.

We were consumed by your care, so I didn't at that moment process the portent of the Home Slice handshake. It took me a long time, not until about a week after your funeral, to realize the significance of your actions. Lisa and I were talking when it became crystal clear. We were discussing the last time you were conscious in the hospital, and I started describing the handshake.

Suddenly I stopped in mid-sentence; a warm rush consumed my face as tears started to flow. My sense of clarity on that night nearly took my breath away. I felt the pressure of impending heart failure in my chest, so tremendous that I thought I would stop breathing that moment.

"My God, my God, he knew!" I believe in my heart you knew you were dying, Bran. And with the handshake that was our routine ritual, you were saying goodbye to me. You said goodbye to me over and over again with your eyes locked on mine.

I'm still overpowered with anguish when I think about that night and the fact that you were completely aware that you were dying. You knew, Bran, that you were leaving this earth. And you were trying to tell me, "Okay, Home Slice, I'm out." What I remember most about that moment is your remarkable sense of calmness. You showed no fear. You just held your gaze focused on me. Bran, when you were a baby, your granny often said, "This boy never takes his eyes off you." You left us, never taking your eyes off me.

Our neurosurgeon arrived to examine you. We were all sitting in the hallway outside your room. I looked up to see our neurosurgeon and his physician assistant approaching. Their slow, deliberate pace and solemn facial expressions caused my stomach to knot.

Our neurosurgeon explained that, based on his diagnosis, you had experienced another significant bleed. The bleed caused increased brain swelling. Your intracranial pressure (ICP), which is supposed to be below 20, shot up to 140. Your brain had become swollen to the point that it was not receiving proper blood flow and oxygen. Our neurosurgeon told us they needed to place you in an induced coma because your condition had deteriorated. The coma would slow your body's metabolism and allow your brain a chance to heal. They also placed you on a ventilator.

I asked our neurosurgeon what your chances for survival were, hoping he would allay my concern. He replied, "Ten percent."

"No, no, no, this can't be!" I screamed at him. I felt someone's arms around me preventing my fall. There were muffled cries from others coming from all directions.

Hearing those words left us in indescribable pain and despair. The words "ten percent survival" reverberated in my head, bouncing off every corner of my very being. In an adjacent hallway outside your room, many friends and family members were gathered, more than I can remember, seemingly filling the hallway from wall to wall. We all sobbed. Our hearts were broken. It was the last night we saw you conscious.

While I sat motionless, attempting to ignore the ache of my body, a memory emerged. It was 1989, and you were three months old. It was your first visit to the pediatrician we had selected after interviewing several other doctors. Your pediatrician was meticulously conducting the examination when I noticed that he listened to your chest sounds repeatedly. Three times he pressed the stethoscope against your bare chest and back.

My anxiousness was apparent, so he calmly turned to me and said, "Brandon has a heart murmur, but I don't want you to worry.

It's very common in infants. They normally grow out it, but I want you to take him to Children's Hospital for tests."

Later at your granny's house, she was not alarmed. I recall her words, "Connie, he is going to be fine. God did not make you wait this long to have this baby to now take him from you." Your innocent heart murmur did go away. Now, years later, I found myself yearning for my mother's encouragement.

That night in the hospital, as your dad and I slept on a cot next to your bed, Lisa sat in a chair nearby reading and studying her Bible, intently awake, as I drifted in and out of sleep. She stayed until 4:00 a.m. She did not say what she was thinking, but after you were gone, Lisa wrote this poem.

I longed to see your right-handed wave from the hospital bed.
Your last goodbye to me.
I wanted to be there with you ... not ask anything of you.
Not ... how are you?
Not ... how do you feel?
Not ... crack any jokes.
Not ... make small talk.
I just wanted you to know when you opened your eyes ...
I was there for you ... for your mom and for your dad.

The next morning, Friday, February 9, 2007, at 6:20 a.m., we awoke to high-pitched alarms coming from the medical equipment in the room. I could see the rapid change in numbers for your blood pressure and heart rate. Your blood pressure had shot sky-high. The monitor recorded 264/160. The whole room seemed to shudder as the sounds of blaring alarms and ear-piercing buzzers bounced off the walls.

I started shouting at your dad to call the nurse, as I rushed to your bedside. At the same time, the nurse was running into the room. "We've called the doctor, Mrs. Spight," she said. "We've called the doctor!"

I held you close, Bran, crying and begging your forgiveness for not taking better care of you. After all, I was that overprotective mom, the one charged with keeping you safe, but I couldn't keep you alive!

Even then, as I felt as though I were losing my mind, there was a moment of clarity. I knew it was time to confront our worst fears and to honor your wishes made clear to us, unexpectedly and quite forcefully, in a dinnertime conversation a few years earlier. I knew it was time to call Sheila Alston for her compassion and expertise. Sheila, a family friend, is also the director of clinical services/organ donation for Gift of Life Michigan. Sheila would know how to accomplish your last act of generosity and giving.

Your dad called Sheila. I don't know what he said to her or what action she took. I only remember her telling me later that she could hear me wailing as she spoke to your dad.

The doctors did what they could to stabilize you, and your dad and I fought to hold it together. The doctors were detailing your current condition to us, as we stood there unresponsive. Essentially they were trying to tell us that there was very little chance of your survival. They also explained that they were required by the State of Michigan to conduct what's called the "apnea test," which evaluates whether the brain can elicit from the body the vital act of breathing. It would determine whether you were clinically brain-dead, that is, whether your hospital room equipment was keeping your heart beating and your lungs breathing because your brain no longer could.

That's when your dad grabbed my hand and said we needed to leave the hospital. We needed a moment to try to breathe, to try to comprehend what was happening. To try to? We went to a nearby restaurant and tried to eat lunch, as your dad listened to me talk out my feelings and hopes.

"Maybe they'll see a sign ... we don't know yet if he's ..." I couldn't complete the sentence.

Your dad and I sat there in tears. He then softly told me what I knew but didn't want to hear or accept. "He's gone, Connie. He's gone."

It had been about three years earlier when Sheila and her husband, Tommy, were visiting at our home. Sheila is passionate about her work for Gift of Life Michigan, and that day she talked in detail about her job, telling us that many African Americans are reluctant and suspicious about organ donation.

She further shared with us that this stems, in part, from the legacy of how blacks were treated by the white medical community. Institutional racism led to the Tuskegee Study of Untreated Syphilis in the Negro Male, in which federal researchers from the US Public Health Service intentionally withheld medicine for decades from a group of black men afflicted with syphilis.

Many African Americans fear that if they sign up for the organ and tissue donor registry, Sheila told us, no doctor or nurse will try to save them in the hospital. We all chuckled a little over that at the time, and Sheila said it was her personal crusade to convince "our people" that nothing could be further from the truth.

"If something happens to him," she said, motioning to her husband, Tommy, "I'm going to donate whatever he has left!"

I don't remember exactly when your dad and I discussed the subject of organ donation again. But it was at the dinner table one night, and you, Bran, were probably thirteen or fourteen years old. The subject came up somehow, and your dad declared he was adamantly opposed to the idea of organ and tissue donation.

"Absolutely not," Virgil said to me. "I'm not going to let anybody cut on you."

But I didn't see a problem with it. "I'll be gone. What's the big deal? I mean, I'm not going to be using them anymore. If somebody else could benefit from my organs, why not?"

The idea of organ donation was not new to me. My mother had expressed to me years before her death in 1997 that she wanted her body donated to science. She wrote it in a letter to me and registered her wishes with Wayne State University Medical School. I think it was a very informed, forward-thinking decision on your granny's part. Your grandma had suffered from many maladies, and she believed her body could have purpose in death as a tool for research and education. When she died, we respected her wishes and donated her body to Wayne State University.

Before that night, like so many families, you, your dad, and I had never discussed what our wishes were for our bodies in death. Death is not a popular conversation around the nightly dinner table.

But as was so often the case, Bran, you made sure to express your opinion. "Why not, Dad?" you asked. "I agree with Mom."

We didn't belabor the subject that night or ever bring it up again. It never occurred to me that I should directly pose that question to you. The purpose of our conversation was to let you know what to do if the situation arose with your dad or me. Never did I imagine a scenario where we would be forced to make that decision about your organs, Bran. But because you had so readily and assuredly agreed with me that night, you let us know that you were in favor of the decision we now were prepared to make on this bleak February day. I knew what you wanted us to do.

During your hospitalization, you had several visits from Reverend Ronald Griffin, the pastor of Rose of Sharon Church of God in Christ, and Father Karl Kiser, the Jesuit priest who was also the president of UDJ. Each time they visited, they prayed for your healing. Father Kiser called me after he was made aware of the induced coma and the upcoming apnea test, to ask if we would consent to have him perform the Catholic ritual of last rites, even though we weren't Catholic.

We agreed, and Father Kiser invited Reverend Griffin to join him. So on the afternoon of Saturday, February 10, 2007, Father Kiser gave last rites, and Reverend Griffin prayed and blessed you.

I stood there watching as your soul was literally being presented to God.

We were required to wait several hours in order for all medications to exit your body before the doctors could perform the apnea test to assess whether brain death had occurred. The test would be conducted over a two-day period: criteria test one on the first day and criteria test two on the second day.

Since the first criteria test could not be performed until that evening, I sat by your bed all day. I watched as a technician put electrodes on your head. As the technician turned your head with what I considered excessive force, I said, "Please don't do that." I watched as your urine filled the collection bag at an exorbitant rate. I watched as the nurse entered your room to empty the bag numerous times throughout the day.

The first test was performed by the resident who had cared for you on Saturday, February 10, at 7:00 p.m. Your dad and I watched. It was important for us to be there. Some (but not all) of the tests to determine if your body were responding included these: You were removed from the ventilator to see if you could breathe on your own. You could not. The doctor pinched and poked your reflexes to see whether you recognized pain. You did not. He took a Q-tip to tickle the back of your throat to provoke a gag reflex. Nothing happened. He dripped cold water into both your ears. You did not flinch. He pulled open your eyelid to tickle your eye with a tissue. You did not blink. He called your name. You did not answer.

During the test, I began to take notes in the notebook I had used throughout your illness, Bran. I was robotic, as if I were taking copious notes for a class and not watching the most painful experience of my life. Soon though, I was no longer able to move as my insides were screaming and pleading with you. "Brandon, please, please respond. Wake up, blink, flinch, frown," I pleaded silently. I hated watching the doctor perform these tests. When he was finished, your dad's arms were around me, ushering me out of the room.

The next morning at 8:40 a.m., our neurosurgeon repeated the same tests. Once again, I stood there motionless watching the same procedure and hearing the same results. Nothing had changed.

This time, after every failed test, my insides grew more and more explosive. I had to remain in control, I told myself. When it was over, I stood at your bedside, Bran, looking down at you.

Our neurosurgeon spoke first. He must have seen the look of guilt and shame etched on my face. "You were a good mom," he said.

Control be damned, my tears began to spew, and my body shook frantically. "There must have been something I could have done," I said.

Our neurosurgeon spoke again. "You did nothing wrong. Remember your son's words: 'No surgery, Mom.'"

I did remember those words. Without them, I know deep in my soul that I may have acquiesced to the advice of a surgeon who had provided a third opinion. On the night our world was shattered after hearing "ten percent," your dad and I had been approached by this doctor who passionately tried to convince us to go ahead with the surgery. I asked what the outcome would be. The surgeon did not disagree with the other doctors who had concluded that Brandon would most likely be left in a vegetative state.

"Why would we agree?" I asked.

"Because some parents want to keep their children here at any cost," the surgeon responded.

After hearing that, your dad immediately walked away. I initially recoiled in disbelief. But as a mom who cherished her son, I understood and realized that I too could be that parent. Bran, you knew I could. Without those words, "No surgery, Mom," I could be that parent.

Your official time and date of death was 9:04 a.m., Sunday, February 11, 2007. You had left us, Bran. You were clinically brain dead, kept alive only by a machine. It was time to pave the way for your ultimate gift. Even though your spirit had left us, the machines were needed to keep your heart pumping until we could donate your organs. It was time to meet with a Gift of Life representative. Sheila Alston felt too close to our family to facilitate the organ donation process.

Once I indicated to Sheila that we were ready to start the process, she handpicked another Gift of Life representative to work with us. Sheila said all her people were top-notch, but knowing us as well as she did, she chose a Gift of Life representative whom she thought would mesh well with your dad and me, Crystal Peeples, who met with us in a hospital conference room.

The meeting lasted a long time, as she kindly and methodically asked us question after question. I don't remember them all, but she did ask, one by one, which organs and tissue we would consent to donate. We only said no when they asked about donating your eyes. We couldn't imagine you, on earth or beyond, without such a significant part of your being. Those big, beautiful eyes were hypnotizing from the first time I saw you and throughout your life. Those eyes spoke to me; they even spoke to me when you were dying. I could not let anyone else have them.

Within hours, doctors operated to remove your organs. The operation lasted more than six hours, and surgeons removed your lungs, kidneys, liver, intestines, and heart for transplantation.

You know, Bran, I don't know the exact moment your spirit left this world. But I know you lingered, and I believe you did that for my sake. There were occasions in my waking hours when I could actually feel your presence and know you were in the room with me: the time I felt your breath on my neck while I read the Bible, the time I saw your infamous cursive "B" on the kitchen stool, and the time I saw you walk into the office/study where you did your

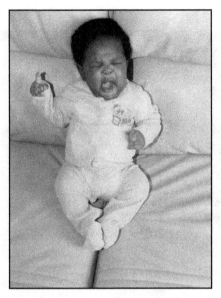

*Sorry Bran, I was a bit fanatical with our photo sessions.
You were growing weary of me at this point.*

*Brandon at only a year old you were attracted to the
game of golf, so your dad thought. I think you saw the
golf club as another toy to add to your collection.*

Your first catch at the tender age of 3.

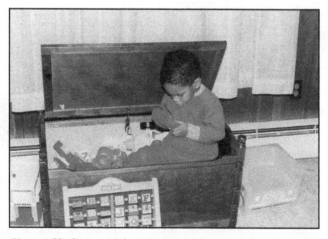

You quickly discovered that playing inside your toy box was much more fun than the cleanup required to put them all away.

Practice makes perfect!

You loved mimicking your dad.

Your first father/son tournament at Palmer Park Golf Course.

As much as you looked forward to the trip to Disney World to see your favorite television characters, you were terrified of the in person gigantic Mickey and Minnie. I can still hear the cries "No Mickey, no Minnie" from my little two-year-old.

You were so adorable in this sailor suit..my feelings..not yours.

Always the entertainer!

*Of all the pictures your dad and I took with
you, these 2 are my favorites.*

A memorable trip to Peeble Beach.

Locked and loaded!

You oozed with pride after making the varsity golf team.

Job well done!

Preparing a video at Palmer Park to send to college golf coaches. I remember how you repeatedly looked at it all day.

Yes Brandon, you were right, real men do wear pink!

"THE BOARD" – *The name you gave your 1999 Ford Escort after a failed attempt by someone urging you to try skate boarding. "That's my board," you told them.*

As usual you were teasing me that day..wearing
sunglasses inside. Thanks for removing them! This was
January 1, 2007, the last 2 photos we took together.

DRAWINGS BY:

Brandon Spight

7

SAYING GOODBYE

In a state of astounding disbelief and days of unimaginable grief, we actually found moments to laugh about you, Brandon.

On the day after you died, your classmates held a candlelight vigil in your memory. Earlier that day, your friend Nick Hammer came by to get photos of you. Your dad and I were really taken aback when we walked into the UDJ school auditorium and saw life-sized pictures of you across the front of the room. The room was packed. Every direction I turned, I saw your friends, relatives, parents, and teachers. For that moment it was heartwarming.

Classmate after classmate took to the microphone to tell stories about you, some of which we heard for the first time! I wish I had had a tape recorder to capture every tale that began with, "Brandon did this …" or "Brandon said that …"

I remember the story one lovely girl in attendance, whom I had never met before, told the audience about meeting you. "I'll bet you never met anybody as fine as me, right?" you asked her. She told the audience that no boy had ever displayed that kind of nerve before.

It made us smile. Right after she said it, we knew it was true because you were confident like no other! "That's my brother. I know my brother," your big brother, Virgil Jr., laughed.

Immediately after the candlelight ceremony, your dad became

overwhelmed with emotion. He put his head down and whispered, "Please get me out of here."

Your dad's buddies acted as his bodyguards, flanking all sides and ushering him out. But I remained and accepted the condolences and hugs from your classmates and friends. What I heard about you that night was only the beginning.

After the candlelight vigil, many of your friends came to our home, your home, where they had been so many times before with you. Your friends surrounded us. As much as they tried to give comfort to us, I believe they found it comforting to be with us as well. They kept coming by the house in the days after you died, Bran, filling the family room to be with each other. They often asked for permission to go and sit in your room.

On Tuesday, February 13, 2007, the entire UDJ school body gathered to mark your passing with a Catholic Mass of the Resurrection in the school gym. Father Karl Kiser celebrated the mass, which opened with the song, "On Eagle's Wings."

"And he will raise you up on eagle's wings,
Bear you on the breath of dawn,
Make you to shine like the sun,
And hold you in the palm of his hand."

Classmate Joe West gave the First Reading from Wisdom 3:1–6, 9.

> The souls of the just are in the hand of God, and no torment shall touch them. They seemed, in the view of the foolish, to be dead: and their passing away was thought an affliction and their going forth from us, utter destruction. But they are in peace. For if before men, indeed, they be punished, yet is their hope full of immortality. Chastised a little, they shall be greatly blessed, because God tried them and found them worthy of himself. As gold in the

furnace, he proved them, and as sacrificial offerings he took them to himself. Those who trust in him shall understand truth, and the faithful shall abide with him in love: Because grace and mercy are with his holy ones and his care is with his elect.

Once again, we heard reflections from many of your classmates. Your golf teammates paid you the most beautiful, unique tribute during the service. Your golf bag was placed near the makeshift altar, in front of the assembly. And one by one, your Cub teammates walked down the aisle with deep sincerity and placed a golf club in your bag. It was a moment of silence that was profoundly touching.

As much as your passing devastated me, your classmates appeared bewildered by the thought of never seeing you again. I think every single young man at UDJ was in line to hug me after the ceremony. The line was as long as I could see. Sometimes I can still feel every hug, and it comforts me now as it did then.

I am also comforted by the words of one of your favorite teachers at UDJ, even though she wasn't really your teacher at all. But UDJ Spanish teacher Wheatley Coleman's memories of you illustrate how you touched so many people in unexpected ways. She tells her story better than I can.

Dear Mr. and Mrs. Spight,

I began my teaching career at U of D Jesuit. I had no classroom of my own, so I hauled my wares from room to room and floor to floor to facilitate my Spanish lessons. Needless to say, my days were exhausting. I frequently finished my last class of the day feeling drained physically and mentally. It was in this state of exhaustion that I came to know Brandon.

Now Brandon was not actually enrolled in any of my classes, but he had a way of showing up in random sections of mine at different points in the day. He and his friend Jordan Redditt would slide into one of my many rooms prior to my arrival, with their collars pulled over their faces trying to blend in with my actual students. Of course, neither of those faces with their bright, mischievous grins could simply blend in. In my mind and heart, both Brandon and Jordan lit up whatever space they were in. They also developed a routine of stopping by at the end of the school day, saying they were there for Mods 17/18 (of course there were no Mods 17/18), but those cheerful visits immediately brought my spirits back up.

Many times Brandon stopped by alone and pepped me up by making me laugh. This was typically at the end of the day when I felt most exhausted and when I would be mentally questioning my abilities as a teacher. "What grade do I have in here?" he would ask or say, "Ms. Coleman, this is my favorite class!"

"You don't have my class, Brandon," I said. To which he responded, "I know. That's why it's my favorite!" with that big smile and twinkle in his eye.

I realize that Brandon didn't have a perfect behavior record, but to me he was frequently a light at the end of many tunnel days, a much-needed happy spirit that brought me smiles and laughter from a talented young man who was unapologetically himself.

I just wanted you to know that your son—your precious, exuberant, mischievous son—truly helped me to survive my first year of teaching, and for that I am ever grateful.

I am so glad that if only for a brief time my path crossed his, and I am eternally changed as a result. I still teach, although no longer at UDJ, and at the end of long days, I sometimes find myself pausing and glancing toward my classroom door, envisioning Brandon bounding in full of stories and laughter. While I am extremely saddened that Brandon will no longer grace my classroom with his physical presence, I truly believe his spiritual presence is with all of us as we face the rest of our lives on earth.

God truly blessed the world by delivering Brandon to you, and although his time was much briefer than expected, please be assured that your son managed to positively impact many lives, especially the life of a young Spanish teacher.

Wheatley Coleman

As you know, Bran, religion has always been a complicated concept for me. Even though we were always spiritual people, pursuing a specific religion to practice wasn't a priority for us, but we were Christians who believed in God. You and I often discussed the selection of a church home; however, we were never quite satisfied with the churches we visited. One day you said to me, "It's okay, Mom. I'll find a church I like one day." One day ...

Well, now we needed a church where we could seek God's comfort and hold your visitation and funeral. We turned to our family friend, Reverend Ronald Griffin, pastor of Detroit's Rose of Sharon Church of God in Christ. He agreed to officiate the service but said we should consider another church.

"Why?" I asked.

"My church is not going to be big enough," he said.

"Really? You don't think so?"

"Trust me," he repeated, "this church is not going to be big enough for Brandon's funeral."

He was so right. In the throes of numbness and grief, I didn't fully comprehend just how many people you touched in your brief stay on this earth. With Pastor Griffin's assistance, we moved your funeral to the 1,600-seat Bailey Cathedral Church of God in Christ, on Curtis near Livernois.

It was brutally cold the morning of February 17, raw, windy, and peppered with snow showers. It was as if the whole world had turned bleak, Bran, the day we laid you to rest.

In spite of the weather, we were greeted at the church by a heartwarming, amazing sight. Bran, you always said, "Mom, one day I'm going to be famous." Well, that day you absolutely were! Passersby thought an entertainment superstar, CEO of industry, or a politician was being remembered. One of my girlfriends, Rhonda Mitchell, told me she wished she had taken a photograph of the mourners lined up all the way down the long flight of steps outside the church entrance, down the block, and around the corner. Inside, the main floor of the cathedral was packed, and the balcony was almost full. It was estimated that more than 1,200 people turned out to celebrate your life.

There would have been even more, but I was told that some of the people who were standing in line outside for thirty minutes or more eventually grew tired and went home because of the bitter cold. Others couldn't find a place to park.

Your dad and I rose so often from our seats to greet friends and relatives that we finally decided to remain standing in the aisle. Eventually Pastor Griffin came up to us and said, "You know, we have to start the service at some point." Your 11:00 a.m. funeral service didn't begin until 11:45 a.m. to accommodate the crowd.

I just did not anticipate this degree of outpouring love for you. Everything about your illness and passing had been unusually overwhelming. Numerous friends and relatives stood together with us in grief, love, and support.

But our friend Sheila Alston shared an insight with me that helped me understand. "Connie, we all have friends that have kids, and they're your friends' kids. But Brandon was your kid, who was also a friend to your friends." She further clarified that they had a relationship with Brandon too. "He was not just yours and Virgil's child."

Her words resonated with me. When we raised you, you were always given an opportunity to communicate directly with adults. You always had a voice in the room, and we encouraged it. Maybe it was your "only child" personality. We never told you to just sit there, to "be seen and not heard." So when Sheila said that you had a personal relationship with all of us, adults and peers alike, I had to agree, "Yes, he did."

That conversation with Sheila brought to mind another special relationship you had with Mrs. Elizabeth Leary, the weekend receptionist at Prudential when I worked there as a real estate agent. Everyone in the office affectionately called her "Bets." You would accompany me on the weekends initially at my insistence. I felt it provided a good study environment; however after meeting Bets, your time there was spent engaging in endless conversation with her.

On one particular Saturday afternoon you said, "Mom, I have to go see Bets with you so I can give her my picture."

"That's Mrs. Leary to you!" I quickly corrected.

After you passed, Bran, Bets was visibly distraught and shared with me the following. She told me that her relationship with you had truly touched her heart, and she felt blessed to have known you. The two of you had something very precious in common. Her husband was a teacher at UDJ before his untimely death. So your conversations about school and the golf team had special meaning for her. She also told me that she was honored when you gave her the picture of you kneeling with your team bag and clubs. She said she carried that picture in her wallet, along with her grandchildren.

Bran, your personal statement as well as tons of photos were printed in the program. Your co-mom, Auntie Carol; your second mom, Auntie Cheryl; Lisa; and your godsisters, Kezia and Melita, worked tirelessly to complete a draft of the program to submit to the printer. I'm sure you know that they did you proud!

During the service, Lisa addressed the congregation to read aloud the personal statement you had prepared for your college applications. But before reading it, she had these words to say, "In the book of Isaiah 49:14, God's children, the Israelites, thought God had forsaken them and forgotten them. But the Lord said … I will not forget you. See I have engraved you on the palm of my hand. You are in His Hands … He will comfort you" (Isaiah 49:16).

After the prophet Isaiah's words, Lisa added a few of her own. "Brandon has often been described as personable, sociable, and full of life. These traits were part of his many God-given talents. But Brandon also had the strength of character and the courage to be true to himself and to pursue his dreams, regardless of what others may have thought of him.

"We honor Connie and Virgil, for they loved and encouraged their son. They gave Brandon the support and tools that all children and young people need to believe in themselves and to pursue their dreams. When God puts a child or a young person in your path—whether for a long time or just for a short while—encourage them, help them, pray for them."

Lisa asked those attending to listen carefully as she read your personal statement and asked them to read it again from the printed program. It was one way to honor you, Bran, she suggested.

"As you listen to Brandon's word, listen. Really listen. And at a later time, read it again and again until you commit to loving and supporting the children and young people in your life."

Bran, I wasn't sleeping much that week before your service. I recall one morning before daybreak hearing these clear and commanding words continuously in my head, *"You gave me life. You gave me joy. You gave me life. You gave me joy."*

I slipped out of bed and began to write my thoughts about you. After finishing, I knew I would read them at your service. Some of our friends and even your dad attempted to discourage me. They thought I should designate someone to read for me.

"Either my voice or nobody's," I told myself. This is what I wrote, and this is what I said to you, Bran. Did you hear me?

Brandon, Brandon, our beautiful boy.
You gave us life. You gave us joy.
How could we know that your body was not perfect from the start?
That those big, engaging eyes would only shine for a short time?
That all your dreams would not come true?
Brandon, Brandon, our courageous boy.
You gave us life. You gave us joy.
We loved so hard and often wished we could keep you close forever.
But you were meant to spread your wings and extend to lives we never knew.
Extend to hearts deserving of your love, deserving of your gifts.
Brandon, Brandon, our courageous boy.
You gave us life. You gave us joy.
How do we go on without you here?
The absence of your laughter, your jokes, your taunting,
The emptiness we feel is impossible to bear.
Brandon, Brandon, our loving boy.
You gave us life. You gave us joy.
We are forced to accept that which shall never be,
Like seeing your education complete or the start of your career
Or seeing you with your lifetime mate and children of your own.
Brandon, Brandon, our beautiful boy.
You gave us life. You gave us joy.
We continue to try to understand that God must have another plan,
That our time with you was decided from the beginning.

So let us say goodbye for now and pray that one day we will once again take your hand.
Brandon, Brandon, our beautiful boy.
You gave us life. You gave us joy.

8

SO NOW WHAT?

You can view yourself as a pillar of strength and believe in the old adage to "Never let 'em see you sweat." Or use "Showtime" as your mantra to get you through the rough and unexpected challenging chapters of your life.

It's important to appear to the outside world that you're on your game. "Showtime!" You remember that, Bran? It was what your dad and I said when we were asked to speak or make a decisive act. It's what we taught you to say as well before a test at school, as you approached the stage for a violin concert, when you ran onto the field for a baseball game, took the basketball court, and, of course, when you approached the first tee on a golf course.

But there is always that one incident that can break you and tear off all the layers of strength you spent years to develop. That was you leaving me, Bran.

When you're overcome by bone-crushing, all-encompassing grief, Bran, you don't know where to turn or what your next move should be. It's as if you're trapped inside your shock and anguish or drowning in unforgiving and overpowering waves of grief, unable to fully inhale a breath of air.

In public, I successfully put on a pretend face. At least I think I was successful. But there were times when I was home alone that my grief and my need to remain strong were not in agreement. In the early days, I would often sit or lay in a semi-comatose state, which I later identified as a state of grief paralysis. The paralysis would often evolve to a feeling of warmness around my face and neck, tightness in my chest, and stinging in my eyes before tears started to stream down my face. An episode, I called it, some more intense than others. Afterward I would revert to my previous state of paralysis.

These periods of paralysis became all too familiar and common for me. Your dad would interrupt these self-pity sessions by literally forcing me to get out of bed, shower, get dressed, and go out of the house, most often to take me to lunch or dinner. So I suppose I can blame your dad for the twenty-five pounds I gained!

As a child, I remember your granny always saying when someone died, "Look at all the people coming over to sit with the grieving, bring food, and offer support. But where are all the people after the service and burial, when the bereaved go home to possibly an empty house or with other family members who are also numb with grief?"

Your granny was in tune with the aftermath. I didn't think much of the impact of grief at the time. But I recall watching her reach out to those in need when all other well-wishers had returned to their daily lives, probably forgetting about the pain of those in mourning.

It brings to mind when your great-grandmother, your granny's mother, passed away. It was 1968. I was sixteen years old. Your granny was overcome by grief, so much so that I too felt the agony of the entire ordeal. To be honest, my agony probably wasn't due so much to the loss of your great-grandmother, but rather to the pain I observed your granny experiencing.

At the burial site after the service for your great-grandmother, your granny literally reached toward the big hole in the ground as if she wanted to join her mother. I could hardly believe my eyes. I didn't understand why she would want to do that. Why would she want to leave me, your uncles, Carl and Clyde, and your granddad? What about her family?

For weeks after her mother's death, maybe months, your granny would sit in the living room in the dark, smoking Tareyton cigarettes and drinking White Label scotch. I asked a few times, "Ma, are you all right?" She would mumble some incoherent words, but I can remember discerning something about how she missed her mama. I know, Bran, you're probably saying that I never told you that! But I'm sure at some point I would have gotten around to sharing that story with you.

During the days after your burial, I experienced extreme darkness as well. No, I didn't sit in the dark and smoke and drink. But my understanding of what I observed from my mother was now crystal clear and ever-present in me. The words "now what?" resonated with me then and still do today.

As I said, your granny was very much aware of the support people need when grief comes knocking. I don't think she received in her grief what she so often gave to others, but I can confidently say that I did.

The morning after your service, after experiencing another sleepless night, I called my friend Adrienne Smith because she had offered to take your photos home from the church. I asked—no, I demanded—that she bring the photos to me that morning. She asked no questions and arrived at our house on her way to work. If my memory serves me correctly, she was going to work early those days around 6:00 a.m., so I'm not sure if it were even daybreak yet when she arrived with the photos. I offered a halfhearted apology, saying something about waking up in a panic and I just had to see your face on those photos. She wasn't angry with me though. I think she understood.

Before Adrienne arrived, I had been wiping the breakfast room table with Windex. She asked whether I been cleaning. "Yes," I said.

I had to busy myself until she arrived because sitting idle was my worst enemy. I bet she was late for work that day because she stayed with me for quite some time.

You loved Adrienne. The two of you had this obsession with the annual Freedom Festival fireworks in downtown Detroit ahead of the Fourth of July. Adrienne said she told you at the last fireworks event you two attended that the next year, she expected you to drive since you'd have your license by then. Of course, that didn't occur. She wrote you a letter of her memories.

Dear Brandon,

I had a pair of white pants with a black stain on one leg after I fell chasing you at a golf outing. I think you were more surprised that I almost caught you than you were at the fact that I gave chase in the first place. I don't even remember why I was chasing you. You were always underestimating the "old folks."

When we first started golfing together, I was playing better than you. You hated that. It didn't last long. I have to give you credit for not rubbing it in. I'm not very technical about golf. I just like to walk and hit the ball, but I can recognize a sweet swing when I see one, and you had that.

Once when you were younger (around three or four), we were all having breakfast in my apartment during the Christmas holiday. You started playing with my thirty-six-inch Raggedy Ann and Andy dolls. You talked to them, leaned on them, and positioned them into different positions. I considered making an Andy for you, but Connie didn't think Virgil would like you playing with a doll, even if it were male and as big as you. Oh well.

I often think about the Scrabble games we played during our New Year's Day brunch. I was waiting for the day when you finally beat me. It happened to my mother and grandmother, so I was sure my day was coming. At our last brunch, you were not feeling well, so we didn't play. It never entered my mind that we would never play again.

I don't know how I convinced Connie to let me take you to the fireworks without her. She did try to make me provide an itinerary, but with the heavy traffic that was difficult to do. Although I tried to restrain myself from swearing around you, I often cut loose while driving. I would hear you sniggering in the back seat because you knew your mother was always telling me to stop. I still can't believe you told on me! When you got your driver's license and a car, I figured you could drive and I would just chaperone on our next trip to the fireworks. That way I wouldn't need to swear; you would. I wouldn't have snitched on you.

I remember the patience you exhibited when you were tutoring Kaylynn with her French. I can still see you looking up at her and asking, again, "How old did you say you were?" I smile while thinking of it. She was younger than you and taller, and I don't think that sat well with you.

At your funeral, I was reminded of attending the funeral of my cousin who lived in Virginia. I listened to people talk about things she had done, and I was surprised. I had never heard about any of the things they were discussing because I didn't know her that well and her many accomplishments were never discussed by my relatives. I heard a lot of things about you, but none of them surprised me because I did know you and your heart. I miss you and the man I'm sure you would have been.

Love, Adrienne

February was always the month your dad took his annual golf trip with the guys. Well, of course the year that you left us, in February, he canceled his trip.

About a month or so later, your dad's friend Walter Watson (Mr. Watson, as you always respectfully called him, even though you affectionately called his wife Auntie Vicki) invited your dad on a golf trip. Bran, I have a story to tell you about your Auntie Vicki, but I'll tell you later.

Your dad was considerate enough to ask me if I were okay with him going. The voice in my head was saying, "Absolutely not! We just buried our son! How could you possibly consider going?"

But the fact that he was asking, that we were even having the conversation, told me that he wanted to go—maybe needed to go. He was concerned about leaving me, but I recognized that he too was grieving. I heard my outer voice saying, "Sure, go. I'll be fine."

So he went. Now, Bran, you and I spent many nights in the house alone when your dad would go on golf trips, and I never felt afraid or lonely then. But this felt different. Without you there, the house felt desolate and unfamiliar. I just couldn't go upstairs and sleep in my bedroom. My plan was, therefore, to sleep in the family room downstairs. By some instinct, my cousin Gwen Arrington called, probably just to check on me. But when she discovered that your dad was out of town, without hesitation she said, "I'm coming over."

We watched TV and talked. I cried. She consoled. She stayed all night, sleeping on the other couch next to me in the family room. Gwen always says that we are not just cousins, we are also very close friends, and she is right. I was so grateful for her company that night.

So getting back to your Auntie Vicki. Everyone was trying in their own way to come to terms with losing you. One day very unexpectedly, your Auntie Vicki came by. She could tell I had been crying as soon as I opened the door, not that it took much those days. She immediately broke down too. She said she had felt the need to come over. We tried our best to console each other and eventually reminisced about golf outings with you. She shared with me that it had been stressful for her to golf at the Detroit Golf Club, where she and Mr. Watson were members, because she was reminded that your school golf team played there as well.

One of her fondest memories, which still today makes her smile, is when she misses a putt she could easily make. She says she can hear your words, "Auntie Vicki, Auntie Vicki!" in that "You know you should have made that putt" tone of voice.

Bran, do you remember how you and your godsister Kyra would always remark how long your Auntie Cheryl and I would talk on the phone? You guys would meander in and out of the rooms we happened to be in, often commenting, "You're still talking to Auntie Cheryl/Auntie Connie?" Well, when we talked, it was for hours because our conversations were so infrequent. Between careers and family, who had time to make social calls?

That changed after you left us. Your Auntie Cheryl talked to me every single day for a year. It was either making a phone call, coming to the house, showing up where I was, or taking me to a meeting with Compassionate Friends, a monthly support group for individuals who have lost loved ones.

I never expected the daily conversations with Cheryl, but I'm sure you're not surprised. After all it was you who so often teased us about our marathon conversations. I looked forward to these talks because it's one of the few times that my mask was removed. Our conversations usually began with the normal chatter like, "How was your day? What did you do?"

But one day I think Cheryl sensed I was different somehow, and I found myself confessing to having one of my episodes.

"So how do you feel when it's starting?" she asked.

I hesitated. My first instinct was to lie. I wasn't sure I wanted to reveal these feelings, not even to her. After what seemed an uncomfortable silence, I responded, "It depends."

"Sometimes it's the loneliness, sadness, or just fear, but mostly it's the feeling of intense rage," I continued. "Then it changes to shame. I think, how dare I feel this way? Just who do I think I am? I am no better than all the others who have felt this overwhelming sense of abandonment.

"The emotional struggle transforms to physical discomfort. I begin to feel warm beads of perspiration on my forehead; it progresses to a burning sensation to my entire face, a hammering headache, and an unbearable tightening in my chest.

"I plead with myself to calm down and breathe in an effort to lower my already medicated blood pressure. But any effort to control my emotions only hastens the inevitable. I start to wail uncontrollably and spew words from my lips that I don't believe are mine. I go from room to room through the home I love, which now feels strangely dark and deserted, yelling obscenities and asking unanswerable questions.

"'Don't you realize how dreadfully lost I am without him?' I scream to the air. 'Do you even care? Where the hell are you?' I find myself longing for and ironically expecting a response, intellectually knowing it will never come."

"So how do you come out of it?" Cheryl asked after listening patiently.

Once again, I hesitated. "I'm not really sure," I whispered. "My arms surround an unmovable body, seeking comfort. A paralyzed state of being that is all too familiar these days. Eventually the paralysis diminishes and mobility resurfaces. I look at the many photos of him (you, Bran) that surround me and begin to sob again.

"I say, 'I'm sorry. Please forgive me.' I grab whatever is near to clean my stained face and try to remember what I was doing. I catch my face in a mirror. I pause, checking for evidence of red eyes or puffiness. I find neither. I think to myself, *No one will ever know.*"

As much as I needed and looked forward to your Auntie Cheryl's calls, I eventually encouraged her to stop calling so often. I felt it was unfair for her to remain so enmeshed in the devastation of my grief and also because I believe that her memories of losing her infant son years ago were resurfacing and having a negative effect on her. Losing a child—no matter how young or old they are, whether there are other siblings, and no matter the circumstances of death—is an unforgettably painful experience. I'm not sure you ever knew about your Auntie Cheryl's son, your godbrother, Bran. His name was Wesley.

The first time Auntie Cheryl held you was a milestone for her. Auntie Cheryl was visiting us, and our doorbell rang. Without much thought, I handed you to her. When I returned to the kitchen, she was holding you close while tears streamed down her face. I realized that the painful memory of losing her son must have forced its way back to that space in her heart. I reached out to take you, but she wouldn't let go. You and your Auntie Cheryl created a bond that day, one that lasted your entire life.

Here are some of your Auntie Cheryl's thoughts and memories:

I met your mom in our tenth-grade geometry class at Mumford High School in Detroit. I called her the "old lady" because she was already fifteen. and I hadn't had my birthday yet. She was always so smart, always did her homework, and wise beyond her years (even at our young age). We became best friends.

I love your mom's big heart and giving spirit. I was so excited when your mom became pregnant with you, and as I watched you grow up, I saw you carry your mom's same big heart and giving spirit.

You and I shared a very special relationship, Brandon. I lost an infant son two days after his birth. I could never bring my own son back, of course, and when you were born seven months later, I felt that I'd been given a second chance to have a son. I loved you as my own. Your mom and I would spend hours on the phone as you were growing up, usually sharing funny little stories about you and your godsisters and discussing how proud we were of all of you. I loved the way you called my name in that urgent, rapid-fire way of yours, and it always made me smile. Your passing left me feeling so sad, Brandon. I had lost my "son" yet again. Your passing literally ripped off the scab to again lay bare a broken heart. The full weight of the pain of the loss of my own son; the loss of you, my second "son"; and watching your mom in her grief, who some days could barely get out of bed, was so very hard. I understood your mom's deep sadness, and it hurt all those around her to not be able to take that pain away. Even though it wasn't possible, I wanted to share in your mom's deep grief with the hope that, in some small way, I could somehow make things better. I'd call your mom some days, and we would just cry together on the phone, not saying a word.

Your mom and I found our way to Compassionate Friends, a support group for parents that have lost a child. We attended meetings for several months and shared our stories, sometimes feeling sad but sometimes remembering something that made us laugh. It's the little things I remember and miss so much, like you spending time with our family on some Sundays while your mom studied and to give your dad a break. The weekend trip to Michigan's Adventure water park on the west side of the state was so much fun, along with trips to Cedar Point and Florida. You would call to tell me something on the phone or how we used to sing the song "Air Force Ones" by Nelly. You were so surprised and pleased that I knew the words! I miss your smile so very much.

I vividly remember the day I was sitting alone in the car in the parking lot of English Gardens, a local nursery, waiting for someone to come out and load my car with a heavy item. I heard your voice call out my name so very clearly, Brandon, and in that rapid-fire tone I loved so much, "Auntie Cheryl!" I was startled, caught my breath, and snapped my head around, and in that one flash of a second, I expected to see you. Of course, you were not physically there. But it was you, Brandon. It was you. I miss you terribly, but I trust in God and believe that in hearing your voice, you were letting me know that you were okay, that everything would be okay.

Brandon, as you know, Margaret and Milton Alston are my college buddies from Michigan State University. We are practically like family. They love you like a son. After your passing, they drove to Detroit from Lansing nearly every Sunday to offer comfort and support and shared dinner with us.

It grew to be quite the crew, including your granddad and the Alston and Smith families. We often teased that they should just move to Detroit. I think Margaret momentarily considered it but concluded that leaving "Happy Lansing" for Detroit wasn't a decision she favored. In spite of the miles on their cars rapidly increasing, they diligently traveled back and forth, providing much-appreciated camaraderie.

We have spent almost every Mother's Day together since you left us. Most often we go out to eat, but I remember one year, in particular, the rawness of my grief was too apparent to disguise. "You guys just go without me," I told Margaret. She wasn't having it. Next thing I knew, she and Milton were at the door with enough groceries for a feast. Margaret insisted that this was what she wanted to do! "Cooking is therapeutic," she said.

The following letters to you from Margaret and Milton capture your enduring vitality.

Dear Brandon,

Ever since you made your transition from this world on February 11, 2007, my mission of showing my appreciation and love for family and friends has even greater meaning, as tomorrow is not guaranteed. I also came to respect a chameleon. A chameleon is not fickle, as portrayed by some individuals. You are a chameleon who adapted to situations that would cause discomfort to most.

I do find comfort in knowing that you experienced more in seventeen years than most of do in fifty years or more. With the unconditional love, support, and guidance of your parents and grandparents, you did not let any grass grow under your feet.

I regret that we don't have the opportunity to spend more time with each other. Unbeknownst to both of us was that we would spend our last New Year's Day with each other on January 1, 2007. We did not play Scrabble, the word game for which you and your mother concocted a unique scoring system, as we traditionally do on the first day of the year. Instead after considerable grumbling, we went with the consensus of the group and played Scattergories, a fast-thinking, category-based party game. Obviously a higher power believed it was time for us to step out of our boxes and give someone else the competitive edge.

I miss you, Brandon! I miss expressing my wild side to you without being judged. I miss our intellectual and heated discussions and conversations. I miss us sharing the good, bad, and ugly. I miss your laughter and mockery. I miss your smile. I miss your presence.

Just know that I will always love you and that you will always be a part of my existence. You don't stop loving someone just because you can't see them in the flesh.

See you later,
"Auntie" Margaret

Virgil and Connie, I have mentioned to you on numerous occasions that my favorite moments with Brandon were the times we spent together in your family room or in ours while the adults played pinochle. Brandon and I would challenge one another in a coloring contest. In my personal coloring book, Pooh, I have pictures that we colored to determine who was the best.

After finishing our page, we would sign our names in the corner like world-renowned artists. Whenever one of us completed a page, the other would critique their drawing of choice, evaluating the crayon color used for the character's body, clothing, background, scene, and so on. We provided feedback on the shades, tones, and balance of the color strokes on the page. Most importantly, we paid close attention to who stayed within the drawing area of the character. One's choice of which character to color was always debated and influenced the judge's decision on determining the winner.

Brandon was the unanimated personality of Tigger. Our depiction of Tigger was a tiger whose arms and hands were raised high above his head in a touchdown pose. Tigger proudly displayed the number one on his jersey, simultaneously reflecting to the world that he is number one. This picture illustrates my feelings about Brandon because he resembled characteristics of Tigger the tiger. He was fun, full of vim and vigor. Uniquely different, like Tigger, Brandon was the only one.
Milton Alston

Bran, as you know, you had family who loved you in Chicago too. Remember how your Uncle Carl and Auntie Carol referred to themselves as co-parents? In their minds, it gave them more authority. I distinctly recalled them proudly announcing, "We're not godparents; we're co-parents! We will be directly involved raising this boy!"

Your Auntie Carol never birthed a child, but she had a natural instinct with children, and they (especially you) loved being around her. The two of you had your favorite things to do; one of them was watching movies. You guys watched the movie *Liar Liar* starring Jim Carrey over and over, each time enjoying it with full-out laughter as if you were watching it for the first time.

Your first solo flight was to Chicago to visit your co-parents for a week, at the age of seven. I distinctly remember you grabbing the hand of the attendant while nonchalantly turning to wave goodbye to us as if you had made this trip several times before. Your Auntie Carol vividly recalls walking through the airport with you as you told her all about your eventful forty-minute flight. "Auntie Carol, the airplane did this … and my seat did that … and, Auntie Carol, the lady took care of me … "

Your Auntie Carol worked for and later retired from a position with United Airlines, so she knew firsthand everything you told her, but of course she listened attentively. You were so excited and spoke so descriptively that she recalls a gentleman turning around to see who was making all this chatter! And, of course, as your Auntie Carol put it, "You know he was loud!"

That was the first of many summer trips you made to Chicago. On one visit in particular, you called and said, "Mom, we have a problem!"

"What's the problem?" I asked.

"Mom, I threw up twice!"

"Well, Brandon," I assured you, "it sounds like you got rid of the problem."

After a few Q and As, I discovered that your Auntie Carol was just being an overindulgent godmother. Your little belly was not accustomed to gorging on hamburgers, fries, pickles, ice cream, and candy, all in the same day. Your Auntie Carol felt really bad that you got sick and promised not to allow any more food binging.

While you were in the hospital, your Uncle Carl and Auntie Carol came to visit. Carol came to the hospital only twice: the first time was just too disturbing for her, and the second time, it was because you appeared to be better.

After you left us, your uncle and aunt returned for the service. Your Auntie Carol and I went upstairs to your room, where we bawled uncontrollably. Carol had to grab a brown paper bag to breathe into and bring her hyperventilation attack under control.

Several months later, I visited Carol in Chicago, a trip in which we spent most of our time sitting at her dining table each day reminiscing about you. We laughed, cried, and laughed some more. The one discussion I will never forget is your Auntie Carol thanking me for you and allowing her to be an integral part of your life.

She said, "You know, Connie, you are not like most moms."

I was confused. "What do you mean?"

She continued, "Well, you made sure I played a role in Brandon's life, and I don't see that with other moms. Other moms would have seen me as a threat or would have been jealous of my relationship with him."

I sat for a moment, a little bewildered. "Well, that's just stupid!" It was my job to raise this little guy to be the best he could be! And knowing I couldn't do it alone, I surrounded him with people who would have a positive impact on his life. It really does take a village!

AN OPEN MESSAGE TO "MY LITTLE BRANDON"

Although it has been said that the greatest gift is to fill a need unnoticed, I now realize that experiences shared with you during your brief lifetime were truly life gifts to me.

I never got the chance to tell you how much I loved those big, beautifully innocent eyes of yours. Those eyes were the ones that surreptitiously peeked through my fence as you repeatedly rode your bike (usually without your helmet) around the corner and subsequently reported to your mom if I had company. You did not miss anything!

I never got the chance to tell you how much I appreciated your numerous invitations to join the Spight family for a meal, and although Virgil accused me of accepting and literally running over each and every time, those times truly made me feel special as I appointed myself your "big little sister" and listened to your comments and opinions on just about anything discussed at the table in that serious "man-child" voice. You, Brandon, were truly always the main ingredient that made those times so deliciously enjoyable.

I never got the chance to express gratitude to you for that finance lesson you taught me when I ran out of cash one Saturday morning at Eastern Market and you generously "loaned" me the hefty sum of eight dollars. I still chuckle regarding fiscal responsibility as I recall your inquiries of whether I had your money that same Saturday afternoon, the next morning and evening, and the following day. The lesson: never borrow money from Brandon again!

I never got the chance to tell you how much I enjoyed trying to surprise you on the morning of your thirteenth birthday as I attempted to hang balloons on the garage in the early darkness while looking over my shoulder and worrying that I might get shot by one of your parents as an intruder. Although balloons were eventually hung on the stairwell inside and you were so cool when you saw them, I did notice an ever-so-slight smile when you opened the side door and saw the Happy Birthday sign posted on the fence. I think I was more excited about that birthday than you!

I never got the chance to tell you how much I valued your erudite assessments of practically any situation—your stern response as I assured you on a ride to the golf course that soon your parents would be getting you your own car, your observation and comment to me that I had only made two mistakes while reading at your paternal grandmother's service, and that stern chastisement when you looked at me and begged me in such a serious voice to please stop smoking. I still see those solemn eyes and hear your voice, but (ahem) you got the car. Recalling your concern truly helped me to eventually stop smoking!

I never told you that when I returned to the D and first saw how you had grown so tall that I started crying in the car (Connie fussed and instructed me not to let you see my tears) because I realized that you were no longer my "little Brandon." I never got the chance to tell you how handsome you were as I said goodbye while you were "primping" in that hall mirror. I asked you then to watch over your folks because they were getting old. I realized that although you did not miss a stroke with that hairbrush, you truly had retained your sensitivity as you displayed such an outwardly cool demeanor!

So many memories ... so much left unspoken. I thank you for each of those special memories, Brandon, and so many more, for filling that unnoticed need in me through your special smiles, teasing, and love, but most of all, I thank you for being you!

Always,
Chie Handy

9

A TRIBUTE TO LIFE

It was the first spring after you left us, and I knew I had to involve myself in activities that would provide distraction from my overwhelming grief. So I immersed myself in something that had given me joy in the past. I planted flowers in our yard as I did every year. That spring, however, the water I used on the plants was mixed with a continuous stream of my tears, and the soil took a beating that it didn't deserve. As I dug relentlessly into the soil, my hands deep in His earth, I just kept asking, "God, why? Why?" I dug and cried; I dug and cried for hours.

I went overboard and planted way too many flats of impatiens, begonias, and varied shades of coleus. I needed to feel life—life that I was creating, nurturing, and growing. I was determined to bring life to something. In some strange, inexplicable way, it was a tribute to your life, Bran.

In the hours after your death, I found comfort—even a moment of happiness—when Sheila called to tell me that your donated heart was destined for a fourteen-year-old girl. I imagined the elation of the parents of that sick girl, knowing that a stranger's heart was on its way to save their daughter. I know, some people might think, *Connie, are you weird or what? You lost your son, but you're happy?*

Yes, I was truly and deeply happy, Bran, because you were going to live on!

But for reasons that remain unrealistically unacceptable, Bran, your heart was not transplanted. Sheila called us back and told us that your heart didn't make it there in time. The girl had passed away before it arrived. My God, I immediately felt my pain compounded with losing you and the pain those parents must have felt as well.

Within days of your passing, we received news that your lungs, kidneys, liver, intestines, and heart valves had been successfully transplanted and that the recipients were expected to lead normal lives. That was a generous act on your part, Bran. I'm thankful that you let us know organ donation was something you supported for yourself and others. In your death, you gave others the most valuable of gifts, the gift of life.

We haven't questioned our decision to donate your organs, Bran, even though I did not feel the sense of joy I was expecting. I thought donating your organs might help me in some way, but it didn't. Not really. If the fourteen-year-old girl had received your heart, Bran, I would have felt differently. I'm still glad for all the recipients of your other organs, but I don't have that same sense of you living on. There was just something about that child getting your heart that would have satisfied my desperate desire for you to still be here.

I didn't want to receive letters from the others who had received your gifts, Brandon. I was physically and emotionally a wreck, and each letter would have ripped through my insides like a jagged knife, with a continual reminder of the fourteen-year-old girl passing away. Perhaps if she had received your heart, I might have been more receptive.

The community learned of your generosity within days of your passing. Journalist Patricia Montemurri, who is married to your UDJ golf coach Paul Diehl, wrote an obituary for the *Detroit Free*

Press. Two months after you were gone, she also chronicled our decision to donate your organs in another story for the *Free Press.*

Sheila introduced us to Remonia Chapman, the program director for Minority Organ Transplant Tissue Education Program, also known as MOTTEP. It's part of the community outreach initiative of Gift of Life Michigan, the organ procurement organization for the state. Because of the generous nature that was at the heart of you, Bran, your dad and I willingly support the MOTTEP mission to increase minority participation in organ donation.

Remonia met with us and sought to learn all she could about you. "I want to get a feel for Brandon," Remonia told us, "because I'm looking at these pictures of this wonderful seventeen-year-old young man who was absolutely gorgeous, who was the apple of his parents' eye, who was just about to graduate from high school and had this amazing future ahead of him but is now removed from you. I want to know: who was he? What did he like? What was a typical day like being around Brandon because I'm meeting your son after the fact?"

You know, your dad still has trouble talking about you at great length to strangers, but Remonia gradually endeared herself to him, and he really began opening up about you. I was leery.

"Ms. Chapman, what do you want from us? I've given all that I have to give. What more could you possibly want?"

She answered, "I don't want anything from you but an opportunity to showcase the life and legacy of your son, who was in so many ways a very giving young man."

Well, Bran, I mentioned that it always had been your dream to be famous one day. Remonia had a plan to make that come true. "Let me share your son with the world. I promise I will be a good steward of his legacy."

Brandon, Remonia Chapman kept every promise she made to me.

Your smiling face and your giving heart became part of a multimedia campaign to increase awareness about organ donation in the African-American community.

Brandon, you were the poster boy for organ donation in the Detroit metropolitan area. With our permission, MOTTEP put your face on the cover of an informational brochure on organ donation targeted to the African-American community. Your face went up on billboards in southeastern Michigan and on the sides of buses. MOTTEP also developed a multicultural donor registry and a DVD aimed at African American churches, and you figured prominently in both projects. And Bran, most of those materials are still in use to this day. I've imagined you strutting around heaven in response.

In addition to featuring your face on billboards throughout southeast Michigan, you were also featured on posters in Michigan Secretary of State's offices, and I think your smile influenced folks to check off the organ donor box on the form when they renewed their driver's license. Your image was featured in brochures about organ donation distributed at black churches and among members of black fraternities and sororities. The campaign is credited with increasing the number of people who checked off that box. In the first six months of 2009, the number of Wayne County residents who placed their names on the Michigan Organ Donor Registry grew from 18,000 to 30,000.

I went to a Secretary of State office to renew my vehicle plates, and there was a large poster of you on the wall for the donor campaign. I stood in line looking at you. When I got up to the counter, I told the clerk, "That's my son." In that moment of connection, she grabbed my hands. She also showed me the other material that featured your photo.

As previously mentioned, there's a lingering suspicion among African Americans about organ donation. You've helped change that, Bran. More and more African Americans have become familiar with and accepting of organ donation. The numbers of African Americans who've registered with the Michigan Secretary of State's office to become organ donors has grown in the years following your death. Now, blacks represent 17 percent of the donor population, while they make up 13 percent of the US population, according to MOTTEP statistics.

Registration is important to maximize chances that eligible donors will be able to make their organs available if the situation arises. While surveys show that some 98 percent of Americans support organ donation, only 54 percent have made their wishes known by signing up. Because of the increased prevalence of high blood pressure and diabetes among blacks, which can lead to kidney failure, there is an increased need for donor organs in the African American community. African Americans account for about 13 percent of the general population of the United States, blacks account for 29 percent of those on the waiting list for organs, mostly kidneys. In a kidney transplant, there is an increased probability for a match when the donor and recipient are of the same race because of blood-type antigens.

Registrants aren't tracked by race, but Remonia knows firsthand how African Americans responded to your story, Bran. "I would be talking about this young man, and someone would say, 'I served on the police force with his parents,' 'I fish with his father,' or 'I went to high school with him,'" Remonia told us. "It was just phenomenal."

Your dad and I were in Florida when the billboard campaign was launched in 2008. It felt at times that we were actually in town because of the numerous calls and messages from friends and relatives telling us they were seeing you all around town!

Your dad remembers what he was doing when he saw your billboard for the first time. He was driving south on Woodward Avenue on a trip to a boat store. "I was coming back down on Woodward, and I look up, and his face was looking at me." Your dad's eyes widen with emotion when he describes his reaction. "His face was huge, HUGE!"

"Even though his death was tragic to us, it ought to mean something more," Virgil says. "In his death, he was able to contribute to someone else's betterment. He was a giving kid anyways."

Bran, I asked for and received the list of every billboard location. We took your granddad to see your billboard in downtown Detroit. He beamed with pride even though he viewed it through teary eyes. Your dad and I drove by all of the billboards. I needed to see your face everywhere it was displayed roadside. I needed to see your eyes. I felt that you, Bran, would have wanted me to. And I could imagine your voice asking, "Hey, Mom, did you see the one in Pontiac, too?"

Did I tell you your face was on the side of Department of Transportation city buses? Well, you were.

Pam Weinstein, the mom of your classmate Robbie Dwight, sent me this note after seeing you on a bus.

I was walking down the sidewalk on Grand River, on my way home from work. It was a cold, grey, bleak winter day, and my spirits were low. I drew near a bus stopped at the side of the road and looked up to find Brandon's radiant smile on the side of the bus. Tears spilled down my cheeks even as my spirit soared. I have seen the bus sign many times since, and it never fails to lift me up.

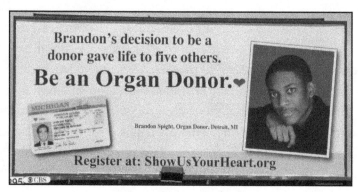

Brandon, your bravery gave others the gift of life.

To Brandon Lee Spight!

What a difference you have made in my life. I never met you while you were you physically present on earth, yet your eternal essence, energy, and encouragement inspire and instruct me each day as I share this message of organ and tissue donation to the masses.

What an incredible spirit you have. What a desire to provide hope and help to people you will never know, but who will forever know you. What compassion and commitment to love and life that you continue to share with others.

I am saddened by the fact that I never met you personally, Brandon, because there are so many things that I would like to say to you. I hope that somehow my words will serve as a witness to these unspoken moments that we now share.

First, I would've said "thank you" for being such a remarkable young man—funny, focused, and a faithful friend. You were a great golfer, a serious student, a meticulous dresser, and a well-groomed young man of destiny. You were a great son who learned great lessons from great parents so you could teach greater lessons to us all. I've learned that you were unselfish with your gifts of time, talent, and self. You devoted yourself to helping others.

I didn't meet you in life, yet you've ministered to me with your legacy and love. Thank you for the opportunity to continue to share the message of Brandon L. Spight. You were a wingless angel who has now received his wings. I pray that our words will continue to be the wind that allows you to soar to people and places all over the world. Thank you for allowing me to get a glimpse of your soul, for your picture is perfect, powerful, poised—your message is purposeful, penetrating, and profound. "Give So Others Can Live"—in life and beyond.

Remonia Chapman, Director of Minority Organ Transplant Tissue Education Program (MOTTEP)

Your story even touched a national audience, Bran. An annual event honors organ donors nationwide. When the national Donate Life office asked Remonia to select a donor from Michigan to honor, she immediately thought of you. When she and Sheila Alston approached us, I felt like it was an act of God-inspired providence, another way you and the Lord were choreographing the impact of your life and death, Bran.

So on New Year's Day 2010, your portrait was among the faces of seventy-six organ donors placed atop a "Donate Life" float for the Rose Bowl Parade in Pasadena, California. You and two other organ donors from Michigan—your portraits created from flower petals, seeds, and plant parts in a design known as a floragraph— were featured on a Tournament of Roses parade float called "New Life Rises." The two other floragraphs from Michigan were twenty-one-year-old Andrew Benedict from Lowell, who died in a February 2008 snowmobile accident, and four-year-old Carmen Lee Wilber of Davison, killed in an August 2008 car accident.

The New Life Rises float had as its main feature the colorful phoenix bird of Greek mythology. The phoenix, consumed by fire only to continually rise from the ashes, illustrated the renewed life that organ and tissue donation provides.

Even though we were 3,000 miles away from Pasadena, the organizers shipped us your floragraph portrait ahead of the parade so we could add our own artistic touches to it. On December 17, 2009, a reception was held at UDJ. School administrators, teachers, classmates, family, and friends were in attendance. As you know, Brandon, since you spent hours with him drawing, your brother Darnell is an artist. We suspect your drawing abilities were inherited from him. Darnell and your art teacher at UDJ, Mrs. Mooney, were impressed with your artistic talent, so I enrolled you in a summer art class at the Center for Creative Studies. You certainly had abilities, but your artistic interests waned over the years. That evening at the reception, Darnell added the finishing artistic touches to the painting, applying your eyebrows and other details before the artwork took flight back to California.

Your dad and I decided not to make the trip to Pasadena for the Rose Bowl Parade. We watched it on TV surrounded by family and friends. As I watched the float slowly cruise down the street with other family members riding along, I was sad that we were not there to witness your larger-than-life image in the parade. But your story went far and wide. You were on the front page of the *Detroit Free Press* and *Detroit News*, Bran, among other publications, and Corey Williams from the Associated Press wrote a feature about you that was distributed on the news wires worldwide. You were called a "hometown hero" in a story by Karen Dumas in the January 2009 issue of *African-American Family Magazine*.

"We have a chance to do something here," your dad told Patricia Montemurri, the *Detroit Free Press* journalist. "We have a chance to make a difference in our community, and Brandon started it."

Linda Williams, a family friend, underwent a liver transplant about a year before you died, Bran. She came to the portrait party and often told us how proud and appreciative she was for our decision to donate your organs. "It's important to get the word out so minorities especially know," Linda told Montemurri. "It's a wonderful show of love and concern for other human beings."

We were fulfilling what, I'm still coming to grips with even now, must have been your mission, Bran. Even though it was a challenging task for us, we were determined to finish what you started. Your proclamation to be famous was satisfied. Oh, how I wish you could have been here to enjoy your star status.

Bran, this is your portrait that was displayed on the New Year's Day 2010 "Donate Life" float for the Rose Bowl Parade.

10

COPING WITH GRIEF

In Michigan, it's not often you hear people say that they can't wait for February. February usually brings bitter-cold, snowy days. But because it's your birthday month, Bran, you anticipated February 21 with such enthusiasm that I shared it as well. Not anymore. Now February engulfs me with conflicting emotions. It's the most extraordinary month for me because of your birth and—excruciating—because of your death. When your granny died on February 5, 1997, you asked, "Why did Granny die in my birthday month, Mom?" Now I'm asking, "Why do I have to endure the loss of both of you in *your* birthday month?"

You learned at an early age to speak to God. Some of that influence came from your granny. As a toddler, you spent many evenings at church with your grandparents. You knew the words to church songs as well as the choir did.

As a child, our ritual was reading a story and you saying your prayers. Your prayers took several minutes as you meticulously named those you wanted God to bless. I would sit patiently as you went through your endless list.

"Mom, a lot of people love me," you would say, "so I want God to take care of them."

I asked you once when you were a teenager whether you still

said your good-night prayers, even though you didn't need me to tuck you in and listen anymore. You said that you did.

Now I was angry with God, and voicing those sentiments was tough for some to hear. In my attempt to seek comfort and understanding, I attended grief counseling at the First Church of the Nazarene in Plymouth, and Lisa and her daughter, your godsister Kezia, came with me.

I admitted my anger at one of the sessions, and the counselor told me that God knew I was angry and that it was okay because God understood. "You're angry because of your relationship with God," the counselor explained. "It's equivalent to being angry with your birth mother or father. Anger doesn't mean you stopped loving."

I felt a sense of vindication for expressing my anger because I had been taught that such expressions were tantamount to blasphemy. So I wasn't crazy or damned to hell after all.

Bran, your Auntie Cheryl and I also attended grief-counseling sessions, designed for parents who had lost children, at St. Paul United Methodist Church in Rochester. The people there were wonderful, kind, and supportive. So many stories were told, and there never was a dry eye in the room.

We would hear over and over how people were grateful to know they were not alone in their grief. But I never quite understood how the solidarity brought comfort, even though your Auntie Cheryl and I attended several meetings that first year. I was, however, amazed at the number of parents who had lost a child, at how many times I heard the words, "Children should outlive their parents."

I appreciated the frankness of the conversations even when they weren't what I wanted to hear. Yes, Bran, you know your mom. I wanted a fix, a tried-and-true technique to eliminate my pain. At one meeting, I received the revelation that what I wanted would never occur. A woman at the meeting announced that it was the fifth anniversary of her daughter's death. She had been attending meetings regularly, and as much as she appreciated everyone there, her pain remained as intense as if her daughter had died just minutes before. She finished by thanking everyone and saying that this would be the last meeting she would attend. I cried all the way home.

When I reached the five-year point of my grief journey, I painfully understood her words. I continued to experience daily the pain of my unimaginable loss. No magic, no pill, no amount of exercise, or no amount of immersing yourself in work eliminates the ache in your soul. It's there, and you learn to navigate it, often displaying a flawless façade. So when the occasional moments of joy make an appearance, you welcome them.

We stopped going to grief sessions after a while. At least for me, I felt like I was being drawn back into my sorrow with every meeting. But everybody is different, and I know others who continue to be uplifted and consoled by the meetings years after their loss.

Within months after your death, my primary care doctor recommended I see a therapist, and he also prescribed antidepressants. I didn't give the pills much of a chance, discontinuing them before the doctor said they could make a difference.

The first therapist I saw cried more than I did during the session. I'd take a tissue, and she'd take two. She was truly moved by my story. I saw another therapist recommended by a friend, but therapy didn't seem to have much of an impact. I think it was more me than either therapist. Maybe I just wasn't receptive to therapy. Maybe my grief was too raw at that time. But as the years have gone by, I see how such interventions over time can help one cope.

God probably heard from me more often after you left us than he had before. If I weren't asking why, I was asking what I was to do. "Please, God, bring Brandon to me in a dream," I prayed. Or I'd ask, "God, just take me too!"

Yes, Bran, from the day I lost you in February 2007 until June of that year, I often asked God to take me from this earth. It so upset your dad that he would ask me, "Are you going to commit suicide?"

"No, I believe that to be a sin," I would respond. I had doubts that God would allow me to join you if I took my own life. In my grief, I didn't focus on who I'd be leaving: your dad, your granddad, our friends, and relatives. I was only focused on being with you.

I stopped asking God to take me. Here is why. I was driving down our street one summer afternoon after a violent thunderstorm. The dark rain clouds had dissipated, and the sky was now relatively clear. I was going to the grocery store, headed north down our street. I hadn't quite made it to Seven Mile when suddenly I heard a tremendous cracking and then a boom! *What on earth was that?* I wondered.

I stopped the car, looked in my rearview mirror, and saw what appeared to be part of a tree. Then I turned all the way around and sat there in stunned silence. A huge tree had snapped off from its bottom trunk and landed within inches right behind my car! Had I driven past that spot a split-second earlier ...

At that instant, I achieved total understanding. God spoke to me without uttering a word. But the message was loud and clear: *Look, quit asking to join Brandon. It's not your time!*

I have not asked God to take me from this world since. What I've asked instead is, "Please, God, when it is my time to go, may I please go to be with Brandon, wherever he may be?" I pray that a reunion will take place someday. Those are my prayers today and every day. So I wait, Brandon, until the moment when I can hold you in my arms again!

Do I wish I knew why you were chosen to leave this life so soon? Absolutely. But I remind myself constantly that no one on earth knows the answer to that question.

Your dad believes you had a higher calling. We were chosen to be your parents because God had faith that we would prepare you for that calling. He finds comfort in his philosophical rebirth theory. Your dad, Bran, imagines you on a road trip across earth fulfilling your duties, and he is at peace with that. My prayer is that God will provide me a similar understanding.

We talk about you and think about you every day. We constantly revisit events of your life with our friends, and sometimes we find occasion to talk about you to new acquaintances and even strangers.

Not long after you died, your dad walked into a Detroit police precinct. Dad didn't know the officer at the desk well, but the officer knew about you, Bran. The officer had a copy of your personal statement, the essay you wrote for college applications that we included in the funeral program, on his desk. The officer told your dad that he used your statement to talk to young people, to inspire them to overcome obstacles and to make a mark. Your Auntie Cheryl's mom, Mama Gambrell, also used it in her Focus Hope classroom. She told us that she hoped your words would inspire her students to strive for success and dream big.

Brandon, even our cat, Haley, felt the dismay of your absence. She would sit and look at the closed door to your third-floor bedroom for the longest time, returning again and again and meowing ever so softly. I would look at her and say, "He's not there, Haley. He's not in his room." My broken heart shattered again and again every time I said it.

My questions for God are the same as they were in your hospital room. They are the same ones you asked me one night as you lay in your hospital bed, distraught and frightened. Your words ripped at my heart then, and they still do today.

"What did I do?" you kept asking. "Please, God, if I've done something wrong, I'm sorry! I'll never do it again! Please, God, let me get better!"

I prayed for God to heal you. So why didn't God answer that prayer? Doreen Odom, the mother of your friend Richerd, assured me that God did heal you, but on the other side. I know you are no longer in pain, but I wanted your pain to cease on this side.

I never believed—and still don't—that He was mad at you. I can't stop thinking, however, that maybe He was mad at me. Maybe I was being punished for some egregious sin by having the one gift I cherished most taken away from me. I blamed myself. After all, I did have surgery to conceive you. Was that a mistake? But as your dad so often reminds me, "It's not about you, Connie. Our time with Brandon was over, no matter how much it hurts us."

Words cannot express how much I hurt or how much you're missed. Nor can words adequately describe the emotional pain I endure every day. My heart aches. But you already know that.

Life goes on, even if my path or purpose is often oblivious to me. I'm in an intermittent haze. Sudoku kept me going the first year. It was a diversion I learned from your Auntie Carol, something I could occupy my mind with instead of thinking about you every moment.

"You've got to pick yourself up and carry on," people kept telling me. Oh, how I hated those words! But what they say is true. Life goes on: I see it playing out all around me. And it makes me want to scream, "But what about Brandon?"

We often take life for granted, never really thinking about how blessed or lucky we are until something happens that changes our entire perspective on life and the reasons we're here. Something unspeakable. Something catastrophic, either to you or someone you love. Then you are faced with how you will continue in a life that took a left turn when you preferred to stay on the path straight ahead.

Believe me, I know. I'm still attempting to accept this horrific left turn in my life. This is my new reality. I refused to call this my "new normal." I will never accept your death as normal.

I don't remember ever questioning death or my destination upon my demise. Was I smug or confident from my Methodist upbringing? I thought my belief in God as a Christian allowed me certain guaranties. I believed that if I were a decent person, a good wife and mother, and never hurt anyone intentionally or never was vindictive or evil, that heaven was my next destination. It was guaranteed. I believed God and I had an understanding, just between Him and me. But your death has fractured what I believed to be inevitable.

Bran, you had a healthy, active relationship with God. You spoke to Him all the time. And you spoke to your granny even more, with the absolute certainty that she was up in heaven, looking down on us and protecting us.

I read a book years ago that spoke about the souls of the dead lingering to comfort the ones they left behind. When my mother died, I suffered through sleepless nights for the first week until she visited me in a dream. It was vivid. In my dream, she called me on the phone and told me she was sitting in a tub—she loved bathing—and that she was feeling fine. Her voice was upbeat, the tone you and I heard when she made her daily calls to us.

I asked God to bring you to me because I wanted that sense of relief and the feeling that you were okay too. God answered my prayer and brought you to me in a dream, but it offered no comfort. In one dream, you were back at home, sitting on the bench in our bedroom. In the dream, I talked to you as if you were heading back to school, and I was worried you were going to try to take too many classes so you could graduate on time. You spoke no words, but your facial expression said, "Mom, you know I'm gone." I didn't understand why you didn't speak to me in my dream, and I woke with a sick emptiness in the pit of my stomach.

I told you about how I prayed for God to take me too after you died. But when you came to me (at least I thought it was you) in another dream, after all my asking to be with you, I resisted. In the dream, I couldn't see you or anything else; there was complete darkness. Someone grabbed my arm and pulled me toward them with tremendous force. My resistance caused us to go round and round in a circle until I finally broke the connection. Upon waking, my breathing was labored, and my heart was pounding, as if the dream had been real. Was it my diminished faith that made me resist?

I wish my faith were stronger. I wish I had no doubts whatsoever that I will see you again, Bran, hug you, and tell you how much I love you. Whenever doubt creeps in, I read this scripture from Psalm 34:18 to gain strength, *"The LORD is close to the brokenhearted and saves those who are crushed in spirit."*

I am, however, convinced that your purpose here was to touch the lives of others and to inspire them with your determination, personality, and courage. I believe that was your purpose, your mission, in that all-too-brief time we had with you.

I have saved your schoolwork, awards, and trophies, Bran, since you were a toddler. I have your artwork from Country Day and UDJ. I have the first scrawls of your name. I have the samples you submitted for the Good Handwriting Award. I have the exams you took over the years, the JUGS you acquired, and the essays you wrote. These are my treasures. No other possessions are worth more to me.

Bran, you grew up with an acute spiritual awareness. Religious seeds were initially planted at our home even though your dad and I didn't have a church home. But I know your awareness continued to flourish and took root with your grandparents' influence. My mom and dad always took you to church. When I read an essay you wrote about faith, I was impressed by your commitment and trust, even at this moment when my faith was being challenged.

WHAT FAITH MEANS TO ME

Faith, to me, means a relationship with God. Faith means how much I can trust in God's will. If a person has faith, it means that the person wholeheartedly believes in something. If you have faith, it means you will give anything to prove and show to others how real that faith really is. No matter what others say, you will still love and believe in whatever you have faith in. Having faith doesn't just apply to believing in God or a religion. You can have faith in anything that you feel in your heart is true. You can have faith in family that they will always be there for you in your time of need. If a person truly has faith, it means that they carry this feeling with them to the darkest of times.

Faith shouldn't just be with you when everything is going well; faith should help you get through the most troubling of times.

I believe in God. I believe that God will always be there for me when I need help. God will always be there when my friends or family need help as well. This is my faith. I trust in God with all my heart. My faith in God is what helps me through the most troubling times in my life. If it weren't for my faith, I don't feel I would have been able to make it through periods of my life, like my grandparents' deaths. My faith in God pulled me through those hard experiences because I believed God took my grandparents to a better place when they died. I also have faith in my parents because faith doesn't just involve religion. My faith in my parents helps me sleep easier at night, knowing that they will always have my best interests at heart and that they won't let anything bad happen to me. I believe in my parents because I love them, and this love developed my faith.

Brandon Spight

Your friend and golfing buddy, Nicholas Bright shared your faith.

Leave the Rest to God

You can dream big dreams
And you can live in the clouds
But there is always something that is going to bring you down
To my knees I fell at the loss of my brother

He could be compared to no other
He was a friend and one that was with me to the end
But the end came too early, and it taught me to take life a day at a
time because it can
Switch sides like the flip of a dime

Believe that your life is going to be long and sweet
Because it can turn sour at any beat
Ups and downs are the name of this game
And that's the type of life you will live by having a realistic mind
frame

I view the glass as being half full
Even with that, life remains cruel
Life is 10 percent what happens to you and 90 percent how you respond
Some days I would like to turn those around

With the loss of my brother, life has always been odd
But I do my best at it
And leave the rest to God
R.I.P. Brandon Lee Spight
By Nicholas Bright, UDJ classmate

11

FOREVER BRANDON

I have often been asked, "What do you want people to gain from this book?" Initially this book was intended only to honor you, to carry out your desire to be famous, and to show everyone who read it what a phenomenal young man we had. But with the passage of time, we have come to believe that the messages we hope to impart have multiplied, that is, messages pertaining to relationships, especially between parent and child; unconditional love; living with purpose; and organ donation. And if I'm brutally honest, I want people who read this book to remember Brandon Lee Spight forever!

Your dad and I sought to raise you, Brandon, as an exceptional individual who would make countless contributions to the world. I felt your outspokenness was an attribute, not a hindrance. When there was a dispute in our family, even though we were the authoritative figures, we provided you the opportunity to freely voice your opinion. Some may view those interactions as controversial, but in fact they encouraged a level of confidence we witnessed mature in you, Brandon. By allowing you to disagree with us, you gained confidence, and we gained insight into your thought processes. Surprisingly, we learned about ours as well.

It's easy for parents to lean on their experience and knowledge and to tell their kids what to do when faced with a problem. We chose to create an atmosphere of listening and guiding that resulted in a shared dialogue to help you become proficient in decision-making. We were not perfect parents, and you were not void of mischief, but we were pleased with the son we created and raised.

We hope the importance of organ donation becomes a topic of conversation in every African-American household. You had the foresight at an early age to recognize the need for organ donation without knowing its profound impact. Your gift not only benefited the recipients, but also the families of those recipients.

How many of us can claim that we made a life-changing contribution to society? You, Brandon Lee Spight, made that contribution to others you never knew. Your contributions are more significant than most of us can claim. In your absence, you continue to make a statement. This is your legacy. That's why we began Plan B, the Brandon Lee Spight Memorial Foundation (BLSMF).

When you died, in lieu of flowers, we asked your friends and family to donate money to your school, University of Detroit Jesuit High School and Academy. We would have been overjoyed if $5,000 had been collected. When the contributions topped $14,000, however, we knew something special was unfolding. Using some of those funds, we awarded the first Brandon Spight Scholarship in the fall of 2007 to UDJ academy student, Logan Pratt.

Your dad and I were amazed. We wondered how we could do more. Mary Barden, UDJ's director of major gifts at that time, answered that question while meeting with us in our home and encouraging us to continue fundraising for the scholarship. Mary helped to produce a brochure about the scholarship and mailed it out, spurring more donations in your honor. I will be forever thankful for her valued assistance! A year or so later, we formed a foundation. The Brandon Lee Spight Memorial Foundation is a 501(c)(3) nonprofit organization dedicated to endowing the scholarship at UDJ. In 2011, we held a memorial golf tournament in your honor to raise even more scholarship money.

The tournament's Gold Sponsor was the UAW-Ford National Programs Center, through its leader, Jimmy Settles. We met with Jimmy, who had heard about you from his executive assistant, Beverly Woodard. Jimmy was impressed with your life, Bran, and wanted to help us help other young men like you.

Carl Rose, the owner of Carl's Golfland, didn't hesitate to make a donation in your honor as the tournament's Silver Sponsor. Your dad often brought you to the Bloomfield Hills store, beginning when you were just a preschooler. In the aisles and backrooms of the store, you found a playmate in Carl. "I'd look up, and my kid was gone. I'd hear all this noise in the shoe department or the backroom," your dad said, "and Carl and Brandon would be playing hide-and-seek."

We had 124 golfers at Northville Hills Golf Club on that beautiful sunny day of August 20, 2011. Due to the tremendous generosity of many donors and the success of the golf tournament, we are currently partially endowed at $50,000. But as successful as the tournament was and even with the urging from all who attended, we found it too emotionally draining to hold another tournament. Because of you, Brandon, and the many fond memories of you, the Brandon Spight Scholarship is now known as a Partially Endowed Brandon Spight Scholarship. It is, however, our hope to provide more assistance to more students by continuing our efforts to fully endow the scholarship to $250,000.

As of this writing, four UDJ students have received the Brandon Lee Spight Scholarship. The recipients are Logan Pratt (2012), Jordan Candie (2016), Joe McEwen (2020), and Daniel Kuzniar (2024).

I remember the first time we met Logan. We were immediately struck by his stature. You would certainly have been envious, Bran. He was at least six feet tall when he entered the Academy. He is now six-eight. The two of you were different in other ways as well. Logan loved science classes and didn't like English. You, Bran, had a passion for reading and writing but wasn't keen on the sciences. Logan is quiet and soft-spoken, and you were quite the gregarious type.

Logan's mom, Elaine Posten, kept your dad and me informed of Logan's progress. She sent us Logan's grades every semester from UDJ. She kept up the practice when Logan attended the University of Michigan, sending us his transcripts and apprising us when he changed his major. She wrote this poem to you.

Dear Brandon,
Although we never met you
Your love shines on us day by day
We have met your wonderful parents
Who although had no debt to repay
Have gathered family and friends
Even while in such deep despair
And given my son a chance
To be a part of something rare
He enjoys the school so much
And he has met many new friends
It is good to see him laughing
And enjoying sports and academics again
This poem is written with heartfelt sorrow
And tears in my eyes
But when we think of your memorial program
We smile and feel joy and pride
The love felt for you and your family
Will always be kept inside.

Elaine Posten, mother of recipient, Brandon Spight Memorial Scholarship

When Logan graduated from UDJ, he was upset that his mom hadn't invited us to the graduation ceremony. Elaine said she worried that we wouldn't want to attend a UDJ graduation since we hadn't been able to celebrate yours. Logan told his mom she should have invited us anyway because it was our decision to make.

So when Logan graduated from the University of Michigan with a bachelor of arts degree in international and comparative studies, your dad and I were invited to attend the ceremony. Logan's invitation touched me. Elaine provided us tickets to sit with her and the rest of their family.

It was April 29, 2017, a chilly, overcast Saturday when your dad and I found ourselves at the Big House, the University of Michigan football stadium, for the bicentennial commencement ceremony. On the way to Ann Arbor, your dad said he was feeling emotional about the day, overwhelmed with thoughts of you, Bran. I provided what I thought were words to calm him. However, when Logan walked up to greet us after the ceremony, I was the one overwhelmed with emotion, unsuccessfully trying to control the tears rolling down my cheeks, Bran. I was very happy that we had played a small role in his success, and really it was just a small role.

The proceeds from the sale of this book will go toward the Brandon Lee Spight Endowment to continue our journey to fully endow. The endowment will bear your name, Brandon, in perpetuity, using the interest earned to finance scholarships for young men.

Perpetuity, Bran. That means forever, God willing. As long as there is a University of Detroit High School and Academy, your name will live on there as being synonymous with helping other young men achieve their greatest potential.

You deserve no less, Brandon. Your dad and I think so, and hundreds of others whose lives you touched and who still remember you with great love and admiration think so too. Your mission in life will continue. After all, you were an amazing son, our little miracle. And you still are.

In the years since you died, Bran, hundreds of UDJ students have passed by a plaque in the school's atrium, around the corner from the gym. Your name and photo are on the plaque, of course. And listed below are the names of some of your former golf teammates as well as the names of Cub golfers you never knew. Each year at the end of the golf season, Coach Paul Diehl bestows an award to the player who best exemplifies leadership and teamwork. He tells the golfers about you. The golf team players choose the award recipient, and the award is presented at the golf team banquet. This is the inscription on the plaque.

"Brandon was a graduating senior and was a beloved member of the University of Detroit Jesuit High School family," reads the plaque, next to your engraved image. "As a member of the Varsity Golf Team, Brandon was well known and loved by all. During his six years at U of D Jesuit, Brandon formed lasting friendships, pursued his passion of golf, cultivated his artistic talent, and continued to achieve academically."

Annually, the Brandon L. Spight award, as noted on the plaque, "is bestowed upon the senior golfer, voted by his teammates, who best exemplifies the qualities of Brandon: Sportsmanship, Charisma, Leadership, and Dedication."

Bran, you gave your dad and me a lifetime of memories. This book would never come to completion if I attempted to include our every thought of you. But one thing is for sure: the memories you left us will forever be our solace. We have shared them with family and friends, sometimes strangers, for years now. Your dad and I not only exchange stories daily with each other, but we often imagine where you'd be, who you'd be, and what you'd be doing today. We cry and laugh. We cry and laugh repeatedly.

What continues to ruminate in us is the nonexistence of new stories. With all my might, I cannot envision a truly happy ending without you in it. These words ring true: *When your parents die,*

you lose your past ... When your spouse dies, you lose your present ...
When your child dies, you lose your future. My future Bran was you!

With this book and your story, we hope that your legacy lives on. We hope others appreciate your foresight to recognize the importance of giving. We hope it encourages other young men to pursue their journeys and dreams. And we hope the Brandon Lee Spight story will spur others to pursue life-changing, life-giving stories of their own.

The grief and pain of losing you remains in the permanent hole in my heart. But the joy of giving birth to you, the joy of watching you grow into a young man, and the joy of our lives entwined and nurturing yours will forever be our greatest gift from God.

Words from the poem "Remembering," by
Elizabeth Dent exemplify my feelings.
Go ahead mention my child, the one who died, you know,
Don't worry about hurting me further,
The depth of my pain doesn't show.

I will love you and miss you forevermore, but you know that.
Mom

12

PORTRAITS OF BRANDON

After your death, Brandon, the letters people wrote about you were gifts to your dad and me. Each sentiment expressed, each moment described, are brushstrokes in a vibrant painting, richly textured with the numerous personality traits of you.

There were soooo many letters. We have included some of them. Some have been edited for length and clarity. As your mom, Bran, I am immeasurably grateful to all the writers for every word, thought, observation, feeling expressed, and prayer offered in your memory.

A MEDICAL OPINION

As I met Brandon for the first time, I was struck by the maturity that this young man showed. Understanding that he had a blood clot within his brain that would need to be treated and that all of the treatment options would significantly alter his lifestyle, Brandon met this adversity with acceptance. Knowing that the cause of such a condition was the result of an abnormal tangle of blood vessels that he had been born with and, as such, was out of his control was frustrating, yet Brandon did not complain.

Because the bleeding was deep within the brain, it was necessary to allow the blood to be reabsorbed prior to proceeding with definitive treatment to the tangle of vessels. During this period, the bleeding increased, requiring Brandon to be admitted to the hospital and to remain on bed rest. Such a challenge is difficult for anyone, but especially for a high school senior who was so active in his school, athletics, and with his friends. However, Brandon fought this challenge head-on and accepted his condition with a degree of maturity well beyond his years.

On the night of his death, Brandon's condition worsened acutely and without warning. Everything Brandon had accomplished—his brilliance, his athleticism, and his very essence—was taken away.

Throughout life, one encounters a vast array of people and personalities. As a neurosurgeon, I encounter people professionally every day who have had dramatic life-changing events. All such patients affect me; however, it is the children and adolescents that are usually the most remarkable.

Unlike Brandon, few of us in our lives will encounter true adversity. Throughout his years, Brandon had no way of knowing that a ticking bomb dwelled within his brain. He proceeded day to day, excelling academically and in his golf. Even in his unfairly shortened time with us, Brandon has reinforced how important the little things in life are, how we must all, each and every day, recognize and appreciate all that we have, friends and family, and never take any of these gifts for granted.

Written by our neurosurgeon

FROM THE FAMILY ROOM

Hey, Bran,

As I pass through the rest of my life day by day, I feel there is a hole inside of me that your absence created. You know sometimes when you lose someone so close to you, you can try to fill that hole with reason and understanding. But in this case, Little Brother, for me it is not understood, and sometimes trying to reason does not work. When I wake up, I feel it. When the wind blows or it rains, I feel it. The hole remains. It has taken me some time to realize what that space represents. It's you no longer being here with us, and the only thing that helps me deal with it are pleasant thoughts of you, along with your bright eyes and the memories and joy that only you bring to our family and friends. I guess I just want you to know, Bran, that every day I try to at least work on it and par that hole, but it ain't easy, man. Thoughts of your bright life and what you meant to my life will never go away. You are with me all the time.

I love you, Brandon, and I will miss you forever.

Your Big Brother,

Virgil Jr.

Is Chicken Supposed to …

My most vivid memory of Bran was sharing a very specific meal together. My sisters and I were staying with Auntie Connie and Uncle Virgil while my mother was out of town on a business trip. I believe this was a Friday evening, and business was being conducted as usual. We'd all gotten home from school and were doing homework before dinnertime. On the menu that night was baked chicken and, I am sure, some kind of vegetable.

As Auntie Connie announced, "Come and eat, you guys," we all proceeded to the dinner table. We looked around, choosing our seats one at a time. Once we were all seated, general conversation began as we began filling our plates with food. The chicken looked quite delicious with its golden-brown color, just as I'd seen on cooking shows. As I cut into my meat, however, I noticed a pinkish-red substance begin to glisten against the white of the chicken.

I asked, "Auntie Connie, is chicken supposed to bleed?"

Well, that was it! Auntie Connie complained, "I'm getting a new stove!" We all exploded with questions and laughter. It was decided that we all were having pizza for dinner that evening.

For many dinners we shared after that, Bran would generally begin his sentence with the now-popular phrase of, "Auntie Connie, is chicken supposed to bleed?"

This was just one of the many memories I have of Bran, but this memory makes me smile every time it crosses my mind.

Jillian Stout Coleman

Dear Brandon,

In this letter, I explain to you that even in emptiness, your absence and with you being gone, you daily continue to live through me, Auntie Connie and Uncle Virgil, Mr. Jackson, your siblings, godsisters/brothers, my parents, Jeff, your friends, loved ones, and donor recipients. Your life, your legacy, shines through each one of us, and the precious memories of you slowly fill up that hole. As a matter of fact, I realize that you were a donor already before leaving this life. You always gave your opinion, motivated others, took time *to give of yourself, connected with everyone through your charm, and shared your talents in golf, art, and writings to the world.*

Brandon, you have changed our lives forever. You challenged us spiritually to think about our purpose in life and to seek God for guidance, understanding, and strength. We are so much better off having you a part of our lives. I am honored and truly grateful having you as a godbrother. I will cherish and love you forever! You are the Gift of Life!

Remembering you always,
Melita Alston Smith

Dear Brandon,

Though you've been gone for quite some time now, our memories with you live and thrive. We laugh and cry sharing stories of our upbringing. We use you as a reference point in family disputes, knowing clearly what you would have said or done in a given scenario. We are sometimes overtaken by grief at the sobering realization that you're no longer here to hug. The absence of your physical form will always be missed, but I am eternally grateful that your spirit lives on with each of us who know and love you. You continue to inspire us, and we hope to inspire others by sharing the beauty of your life with the world.

In recent years, many of us have had the opportunity of sharing you with the next generation. We have children who speak your name, know your face, and share in the laughter and retelling of your memories. Children who would have made you laugh like never before, Bran. Children who insist on having a photo of you nearby and, every so often, want to sit in the blue bathtub that you bathed in as a boy. And though you grew into an amazing young man before leaving this world, part of me never let go of the fun and witty little guy I babysat, read bedtime stories to, and bathed in that blue bathtub. I love you from start to finish … and beyond.

Kezia McAllister

When we were younger, I used to complain about sharing a room with you. I couldn't understand why the girls got their own room and I didn't. But to be honest, those were the best video-gaming years of my life. I wasn't the only one up first in the morning ready to play or do something. You always let me pick the video games, as long as you were able to go first. Besides, all those other rooms in the house are pretty creepy if there is no one else in them. But I guess I should have told you that …

Not too long ago we would spend our afternoons at the breakfast table "doing" our homework. Well, of course, I couldn't really concentrate between the giggling, your mom scolding us for talking, and us laughing hysterically at you scolding your friend whenever he tried to speak to us. I was never going to get any homework done, but I guess I got a lot of life in, irreplaceable life. I should have told you that too.

And it seems like just yesterday you were honing your skills of scolding your friends for looking at your godsisters. Still quite hysterical to us, but nevertheless a varsity sport for you. After the laughs, however, I took a moment to step back and notice how much taller you were and how much more confident you were now—tougher, stronger, more vibrant, and excitable. Although I always thought age played into seniority, you definitely were the big brother. I'm really glad that I told you that.

Erica Alexander

*Words so deep I cannot write
I still have this uncontrollable urge to cry at night
What impact has Brandon made on me, you ask?*

How can I begin to explain the impact of a brother
Not biological, a godbrother, the brother I should have had

Sometimes things happen and God makes other plans
Reasons obviously unknown to man
But God still blessed me with a brother
My second mother called him "Braaan!"

Every day when we were younger was new and exciting
My brother was always warm and inviting
Words so deep I cannot write
The memory of him I often fight

It hurts so much just to say his name
My mind can't even wrap around the pain
Or get over the guilt of not seeing him before his final day
Maybe I'm selfish, but I wanted him here
But I guess God wanted his child, his angel, my godbrother, to be near.
Kyra Harris Bolden

Dear Brandon,

Thank you for all the wonderful memories. Thank you for making me laugh, sometimes because of your jokes and other times just because you were being you. You have brought me joy, love, and many smiles.

You have made many impressions on this world, and one is on my heart. Thinking of your smile makes me smile, and that impression will last a lifetime. Thank you for all the lasting impressions you have made on me. I will carry them with me always. I am so blessed to be your cousin.

Love always,
Brie Cocroft Jackson

Brandon,

If we're being completely honest, I didn't want to write this. Even the thought of writing this reduces me to tears. Writing this means that you are, in fact, gone. They say time heals all wounds, but my sorrow has never seemed to pass.

I don't live my life with many regrets, but there is one thing I have never been able to reconcile. Before you left us, you had been on my mind. Often I had dreams that we were chatting about your college plan. I thought about texting or calling to see how you were doing. And as it happens with so many things in life, I got busy. And a few months later you were gone. So to avoid another regret, I am writing these words to you.

This year I have decided to live my life with more intentionality and to ensure that my actions and my time are an accurate reflection of my highest priorities. And you, my godbrother, would certainly fit into that category. It's nearly impossible for me to acknowledge that I will never be able to talk to you again. Try as I might, I cannot avoid this fact. So I will write these words with gratitude that they have presented the opportunity for me to reflect upon how much I love you and how much you are dearly missed. Anyone who met you was captivated by your confidence and commitment to loving life. Your legacy is an inspiration to all and most certainly to me. I love you.

Whitney Harris Brown

I Heard Marvin on the Radio and He Spoke to Me About Brandon.
By Jeffrey Smith

As I drive down that cold and crowded Interstate 96
I sometimes call out to you, little boy
Still upset about what "went down"
With everyone's little pride and joy.

I asked Marvin, Why am I still down?
He told me to "keep it movin'" bro
Everything is gonna be alright
That's just the way love goes.

Marvin told me, "Brandon knows"
Your friendship was true
And he is happy to know
How sweet it was to be loved by you.

He said, "Jeff, a troubled man always looks
For answers in weary times
Release your emotions because
You got to give it up sometimes."

Marvin, I have to tell you,
I watched how Connie would look into Bran's eyes
As if she were silently communicating to him
You're all I need to get by
She has been strong
Strong for everyone and me
Marvin, I know she is being helped by Bran's
Precious love and memory.

Marvin, I just passed Interstate 275
The highway is so damn crowded, and I feel sad
But I'll be doggone
If everyone around me is gonna make me mad.

Marvin, I'm trying to maintain my sanity
But it makes me wanna holler
When I think of Bran's promising life
Taken from us without a stutter.

As gatekeepers for the Motor City
Uncle Virgil and Aunt Connie
Provided love, guidance, and shelter to Brandon
And were never too busy to care for their baby.

Nothing about him was ever superficial
Brandon is and will always be
100 percent pure SPIGHT
To you and me.

There's nothing like the real thing
And this is what made Brandon unique
You could never say he reminded you of someone
Because he wasn't timid or meek.

We watched Virgil proclaim to you, Bran
As he built his whole world around you
And in classic Virgil style he did just that
Something that garnered admiration from your crew.

God created a life through Virgil and Connie
And brought you to all of us—a little boy dressed in true blue
Do ya know Brandon, you are teaching me to be an adult?
And I bet you never knew

When I feel down
I just say to myself
What would Brandon do?
Love you and see you later.
P.S. You would be proud of my impersonations.

In Memoriam

Brandon was one of the coolest cousins I have ever had the privilege of saying I was related to. Thus, picking a single memory is not only difficult but nearly impossible.

I remember a party at his house back when I was thirteen. We had not seen one another in years but quickly got reacquainted, realizing how much more we had in common than our first names. First we talked and hung out in his room. My brother and I both remarked how huge his place was, but he was humble and merely replied, "Not really." After chilling in his room for a while, we went back outside. He wanted to play golf on his mini-course, but that wasn't my cup of coffee, so we played "brick-ball." He didn't have a basketball rim, so we aimed for a specific, dark brick on his house, which would count as a basket. I nearly broke one of the house windows with my first shot, but I ended up winning 21-18. After that, he quickly suggested that we go find an actual rim to play on!

A school friend of mine, Reggie Dozier, stayed down the street, and I knew he had a rim. So we (Brandon, my brother, and I) walked to his house to play, but he wasn't there, so we had to turn around and go back. On the way back, we saw a huge pit bull that was off its leash and behind a small gate. It began barking viciously at us, and I remember Brandon saying, "Dude, if that dog jumps that fence, I'm jettin' out of here!"

We quickly agreed, but luckily we didn't have to. We got back to his house, played a wrestling game on his Xbox, ate, and went outside to play hide-and-seek in his garden, and then before I knew it, it was time for us to part ways.

Leaving was sad for me because in those few hours I felt I had gained another brother. Brandon was actually big brotherly in personality: he'd always be there if you needed someone to talk to, and being the eldest of three, I sometimes needed someone to talk to!

All the other times we hung out were just as fun as the first, joking and laughing all the time. I remember a family barbecue at my Uncle Jason's house when our cousin, Li'l Jason, got into it with a boy down the street. I tried to separate them. "Naw, man, they're supposed to be friends!" I said, but Brandon told me to fall back. "Just let them fight it out, dude," he said.

So I stood back and enjoyed until Li'l Jason landed a big one on the little boy's chin and decked him. I remember we all went crazy, especially Brandon, and we cheered Jason back to the party while the boy ran back up the street to tell his mom. I know this isn't a very flattering memory of Brandon, but it's definitely one of the funniest and one of my favorites, so please don't think any less of him because of it.

Another one of my favorites was a phone conversation. I heard that he had "wrecked" one of his mom's cars, so I called and slyly asked him what happened. He quickly retorted, "Dude, I did not wreck that car!" He briefly explained how he had hit a curb and the hubcap fell off and left it at that. This may seem unremarkable to some, but his reaction was priceless to me.

I didn't attend his funeral. It was not out of disrespect: it was out of weakness and cowardice. I could not bear to look at him in that casket for the last time, sleeping and peaceful.

But if I could talk to Brandon again, I would say, "What's up, my dude? How you doing, bro?" Then I would reminisce on the some of the good times like the car, the girls, the party—ask him why he never introduced me to Gabby—and, of course, the day at his house. But I wouldn't say goodbye. I would say, "See you later." So when I die, it'll be with a smile, knowing that we'll both be living in that big house in heaven.

Yours truly with love,
Brandon Michael Patterson

Dear Brandon,

For as long as I can remember, I've had two brothers. They lived with me, we saw each other every day, and we shared the same mother. But something happened every time you came around. Suddenly our sibling circle of three became four. It was always amazing to me how easily you could become a part of our circle. It seemed as if you had been with us since birth because you fit right in. I've always admired that about you.

Anything we talked about, you always had something to add, and surprise, surprise! It was always the missing piece to our conversation puzzle. Perhaps the most incredible thing about it is that when it was over, you always left a mark, whether it was the funny things you said, like my favorite expression of yours, "Dude," or your facial expressions.

I remember how we used to laugh and joke whenever we got together, especially at my grandmother's eightieth birthday party when you insisted on stealing my cellular device. No matter what I did, you and my brothers would not give it back! So as my sole act of revenge,

I begged your mother to give you a whupping. I wonder if you ever got that whupping? LOL! Sike!

My funniest memory of you is at a family gathering your mother had at your house. My brothers and I were up in your room playing video games. You were telling us about how you played golf and that you were a caddie. Just being me and acting stupid, I thought about that and looked at you with your glasses and blurted out, "Are you a nerd?" Without even looking away from the video game, you very sternly replied, "No!"

I was so embarrassed because both my brothers just looked at me like, "What an idiot!" Looking back at it now, I laugh, not believing I said something so stupid, and I realize you were the greatest "non-nerd" I ever knew.

All these memories are forever etched in my mind. When I think about you, I realize that remembering you isn't the part that hurts; it's saying Brandon "was" my cousin. So I refuse to say it. You are my cousin, and you have and will forever have a tremendous impact on my life. Thank you for giving me the opportunity to know you for the short period that I did.

With all my love,
Breah Patterson

While attending a conference in Detroit, my Aunt Quincy, Brandon's grandmother, insisted I come for dinner. Afterward we would visit Connie and Virgil in their new home. The main reason really was to meet Brandon, who was about two-and-a-half years old. He was the apple of their eye.

Brandon's dad gave him a set of golf clubs, made to suit his age. He lost no time to show off his golf swing. Even at that age he had form.

The highlight of the evening was when I asked to use the bathroom. His grandmother asked Brandon to show me where it was. Brandon eagerly led me to the next room and pointed to his potty chair. Needless to say, we all had a big laugh. I treasure those memories.

Geraldine T. Evans

He really was my best friend. I could talk to him about absolutely anything and not worry about him judging me or making fun of me. We shared so many secrets that still to this day, I will not tell anyone. I enjoyed every moment I spent with him. Richerd, Brandon, and I used to have these late-night phone conversations. We would be on the phone with each other for hours at a time, talking about girls, boys, drama, music, anything. He would give me advice, and I would do the same for him.

I texted his phone a few days before he went into the hospital. I asked how he was feeling and told him to check in with me every day. I said I would check on him also. He got so mad and said, "Charly, stop it. I'm fine."

I said, "Brandon, I'm not kidding. Every day just tell me how you feel and that you're okay."

He said to me, "Chill out, cuz. I'm straight."

Two days later he was in the hospital. The last time I saw him awake, he was so mad. He was just lying in bed watching TV, and before I left, I gave him a hug and a kiss, and he looked at me after I kissed him and rolled his eyes.

Love you, Brandon. Forever you are in my heart and mind. Miss you, cuz.

Charly Jackson

Dear Brandon,

I wondered when I would finally pick up a pen and paper to write down what I've pent up for almost a year and a half now.

Wow! I miss you, B. I miss your bright, cheesy smile and those eyes that could make the brightest star blush. I'm not sure if you know this or not, but I think about you every single day. Some people will probably say that to make you feel good or whatnot, but I mean it. I've never told anyone that because I don't like to wear my soul on my sleeve, but I trust you won't tell.

I've talked about you to fewer people than I can count on one finger. Maybe it's because I felt like if I looked as though I had forgotten about you, nobody would ask me questions or try to talk to me about you or attempt to sneak the "How do you feel?" therapy session by me.

Well, my plan worked. Nobody said a word to me, and I sorted everything out for myself. Whether that was the right thing to do or not, I don't know. It's how I like to handle my issues. I didn't grow up in the same house with anyone my age, so I've always practiced soliloquy in order to talk out things in my mind.

You were a tough cookie to crack, buddy, but I've learned so much about life in general because of you. That Sunday morning on February 11, 2007, unfortunately was a huge awakening and changed me as a person forever. No longer am I naïve, holding grudges, stressing over petty crap, taking life for granted, and always thinking about what I will do one day in order to change the lives of others for the better. I can look at your pictures of precious moments frozen in time and cry—not tears of sorrow, but of joy! Crap, I'm crying now! More like watery eyes, but I'm steady smiling as well.

You have given me a gift, the gift of everlasting joy in life, and I am in debt to you for eternity! I thank Him for you every time I look at the glass half full instead of half empty. I thank you for all the timeless memories and thoughts you have given me. Thank you! You haven't a clue of the weight that I feel has been lifted off my shoulders by writing you!

Yes, my trip to Lansing last summer was missing a key piece to the puzzle, but every time I stepped onto the golf course, I remembered when you had me point at any object on the driving range and you sent the ball flying directly that way. When we went to the banquet, I remembered how the year before, you were fuming because some of the guys cheated and you didn't win the prize, and we cracked up about it later.

When we went to Maggie Moo's for ice cream, I remembered standing in line with you and pointing through the glass at all the possible flavor combinations and joking around and how we were sure we were going to come back next year. When I hit the pool alone, I remembered you swimming with me just the year before. When I visited my friend, Deyea, I remembered how much you made us laugh and how much we enjoyed being together.

Even though I looked left and right and couldn't see you, I knew you were there. As I finished the last Harry Potter book, I honestly thought of you the whole time. As I followed the storyline, I kept thinking: what would Brandon have thought about that? Every page I turned, I dedicated to you. Every day I wake up, I dedicate to you. Every triumph in life, I will dedicate to you.

I love you always, miss you always, and pray for you and your family always!!

Thank you and until we meet again,

Keli Danielle Boyd

FROM THE NEIGHBORHOOD AND COMMUNITY

I overheard my son talking about a fellow student who had fallen ill. I didn't know who or what, but the frequency of discussion and intensity of concern showed me two things: the connectivity shared by the students at University of Detroit Jesuit High School and Academy and the student, whoever he was, was well-loved and respected.

I soon learned that the student was Brandon Spight, who soon lost his battle, a loss that sent a wave of grief throughout the school and city. He was what everyone hopes for in every young man—handsome, intelligent, athletic, kind, and with a promise of uncompromised potential.

I was writing for a weekly newspaper at the time, and after a little bit of digging, I wrote a column about him and the impact he had on the school and other students. I learned that he was the only son of two retired Detroit police commanders. Brandon played golf, like his dad. He had an engaging spirit and personality. And everyone who knew him loved him.

I never got to meet Brandon, but I did meet and connect with his parents, Connie and Virgil. They are the epitome of strength and class and the apparent source of all that Brandon was as a person. Our conversations were enlightening, each revealing a little bit more who Brandon was and the person he was destined to become.

I believe it is important that no life be lost, even one that has physically ended. Brandon left too soon, with much unfinished in his life and the lives of those he knew.

We began to talk about how his life and legacy could continue. Connie and Virgil established the Brandon Lee Spight Memorial Foundation to provide scholarships so deserving students could have the opportunity to attend the prestigious and acclaimed UDJ.

But there were so many stories to be told, words to be said, and memories to be shared. I suggested to Connie that we write a book. It would be entitled Dear Brandon and allow those who knew him—even those who never knew him—to share their thoughts and emotions. The compilation would also provide a healing platform for shared memories. And sales of the book would help fund the scholarship.

Here's what my entry would say:

> *Dear Brandon,*
>
> *I am so sorry that we never met. I felt like I was going through everything with your school family and never imagined someone I never knew could have such an impact. But you did.*
>
> *After meeting your parents, I understood. You were an amazing young man destined for greatness—loved, respected, and admired.*
>
> *Those that you touched, whether you knew them or not, were left with a major void that we now all seek to fill in other ways. That's what we hope to do with the book, the scholarship, and living our lives as you did yours, with integrity, honesty, and compassion for others.*
>
> *Many are committed to keeping your memory and legacy alive, and I am proud to be a part of that effort.*
>
> *Rest well, dear Brandon.*
>
> *Karen Dumas*

JUST BEING BRANDON

I remember Brandon as a little boy
Cute and playful as he played with my two little girls
He held his own with those two teasing girls, even though he was
younger

Just being Brandon
He grew up and developed into quite a young man
Smart, intuitive, gaining in experience and knowledge
Becoming a leader, becoming quite a golfer
Becoming quite thoughtful, wise beyond his years
Destined to shine as an example to other young men

Just being Brandon
Who could ever know his life would be so short?
Who could ever know the pain his parents would feel?
We thought we had years ahead to get reacquainted again
Then Brandon was gone

Just being Brandon
He is here with us through so many lives he touched
Because of Brandon, others live, breathe, and walk this planet
Because of Brandon, young people who knew him are changed forever
Because of Brandon, young people are attending school every day
and not taking their education lightly
How strange it is too that those two little girls he once played with are
following their paths so similar to the path he dreamed of following
Brandon is living on in so many ways

Just being Brandon
Now looking at the stars at night or
Watching the sunrise along the ocean

I sometimes think of Brandon
Just being Brandon

Kaye Scott, deceased

Brandon, as the child taught me, the elder. He taught me how to have fun with a child. Playing games included laughter and jokes with the hope of distracting me so he could win. One year I went to Disneyland with Brandon and his mother. One day he suggested we go to an exhibit that involved a movie about animals and bugs. He did not tell me that he had seen it before. The movie was shown in 3D, which required wearing special glasses. Thus, it seemed we could feel rats crawling over our feet and bugs flying so close you could touch them and watch as the biggest snake (which I have a horrible fear of) seemed to come off the screen.

I was so scared, jumping and screaming, but trying to act as an adult with this child. But the surprise I got was that, in my anxiety, I often looked away from the screen and noticed Brandon was watching me and laughing. When he discovered that I knew he was enjoying me rather than the movie, he began to tell me what scenes were coming up for me to close my eyes as he continued to laugh.

I raised daughters. There wasn't a young boy child for me to talk to one on one and form a relationship. Then along came my grandsons. My relationship with Brandon prepared me, taught me how to relate to them, and enjoy them. I have learned not to become too upset when a grandson purposely leaves his rubber snake where I can see it. I am enjoying my grandsons, and often I inwardly thank Brandon for having been there to teach me.

Rosalyn Henderson, deceased

Dear Brandon,

You will not remember me because I knew you from the beginning, yep, before you were born. I remember you as a happy-go-lucky, very bubbly little fellow, always laughing and smiling.

I have known your parents for a long time. I must say I admire them both because they are real people. Meaning, they are both honest, clean-cut, down-to-earth people. I met your dad first, working in the same office. He was one of my supervisors. He was a straight arrow, a by-the-book law enforcement officer. He was always a gentleman, never telling those little dirty jokes that the other officers told, just to see the expression on the young ladies' faces.

Your good old dad was always manner-able. He knew when to laugh and when it was not the time for laughter. He could relate to everyone. Even me, an outspoken female civilian in a predominantly man's world, made no difference to him. We were friends from the beginning. And believe me, I did not get along with most people.

Years later, I met your mom, who is just about the nicest, educated, prettiest officer that one can ever meet. She's not full of herself, and she could relate to everybody too. I know this sounds a little bit thick of mush. But from my point of view, you could never have picked better parents. And I can truly say they definitely never could have picked a better son. Just ask them!

When your mom had surgery in order to conceive you, I visited her at the hospital. The day I went to the hospital to see your mom is one of the most memorable moments in my life. I went to visit her, you know, to make her laugh and wish her well.

Well, let me tell you. I rushed into her room with a smile in my heart and a big grin on my face, humming a song and feeling really good about everything in life and bam! There she was with needles and tubes everywhere. I am not often at a loss for words, but there I was. I didn't know what to think or say.

I had to act as if I were not shocked. I hoped she didn't notice that all the blood drained from my head and went down to my feet. But I was cool. I didn't pass out. Needless to say, from that day forward when I visit anyone in the hospital, I go with a different attitude.

I was at your home-going service and have since gone to your final resting place with your mom to plant hostas. I look forward to visiting you again.

From a deceased friend

In our University District neighborhood in northwest Detroit, Brandon was a popular presence. I saw Brandon's dad ambulating in his backyard and decided to make a neighborly visit. His dad was in the yard with a pitching wedge, chipping golf balls at a ten-inch flowerpot about fifteen yards away. While I stood there watching him miss that pot with great consistency, Brandon came out of the house and joined us. I asked his dad if I could see the wedge. Then I turned to Brandon and told him I'd give him a few pointers. (I've never hit a golf ball in my life.) So I shuffled my feet, wiggled the club, told Brandon to keep his head down and his elbow straight, and took a practice swing.

Brandon, in the fashion of a grand and noble gentleman, asked for the club, set a ball on the lawn, positioned his feet, and explained that he would turn his body slightly to the left and open the face of the club. Then he chipped that ball neatly into that flowerpot fifteen yards away and returned the wedge to me. He asked, "Like that?" I calmly replied yes and complimented him on being such a quick learner, and I handed the club back to his dad with a "hey, dude" look. His dad, in turn, replied with the "oh well" shrug while silence prevailed. Needless to say, the party broke up.

Ken Jones, neighbor

I was smitten with Brandon. He was funny and easy to talk to. Unlike so many young people who have only one-word answers and no time for conversation, Brandon would engage you in a running dialogue.

We once talked about the young girls that grew out of the cracks in the sidewalks: these unique creatures appear whenever a young man obtains a driver's license. They become uncontrollable and quite a nuisance when he receives his first car. I had already observed a few of these creatures who found it necessary to stop in front of my house for up to a half hour, talking to each other as they looked across the street, hoping to see Brandon or for Brandon to see them. I knew where they lived and told him to watch out for these cuties. I was going to protect him from … I don't know what. I wanted to watch him graduate, go off to college, and live the perfect life that he was well on his way to having.

I called myself protecting him on another occasion when I snitched on him. My husband and I were returning home, and just as we were slowing to turn into our driveway, Brandon backed out of his yard and into the street without stopping to check traffic. I told Connie. I did not want him to become one of the grim statistics that befall young drivers. I was sure Virgil and Connie would make sure he did not make that bad move again.

A week or so later, I went across the street to talk to Connie. Brandon was in the kitchen. He mumbled and barely acknowledged my presence. It was not like Brandon to act like that. It would not have surprised me if he had chided me for being a tattletale. I would have pretended to be remorseful if he had told me his parents had given *him heck for driving recklessly. I would have insincerely apologized as I told him if it happened again, I would tattle again. I thought he was angry, and I was willing to wait until he got over it because all I wanted were for him to be safe. Now I know that he was already having headaches. He had bigger problems than a nosy neighbor snitching. I will forever miss him.*

Diane Jones, neighbor

"What a charming young man." That's how I remember Brandon. He could really put it on his mama (and his daddy, too, although Virgil won't admit it). I remember walking the neighborhood with Connie to check on one of our real estate properties. Connie was so proud of Brandon for "taking her orders" to read and not leave the house until he was done. Maaaan, just as Connie finished that sentence, here comes Brandon whisking around the corner in his red car, flashing his charming smile, work undone! This was funny only because Brandon knew how far to push the envelope with his mom—not out of disrespect, but with charm. He finally got that assignment done!

Virgil allowed Brandon's charm to melt his heart too. I remember a time when Brandon shouldn't have had company and Virgil covered for him. As Connie and Virgil returned home, Virgil gave Brandon a "head's up" upon their return … and thought Connie was "slow," not catching on to that one.

Rhonda Mitchell

I didn't know your Earthly soul
In Spirit you illuminate the Universe
Lighting up the hearts of those
You would have never touched
As you inspired a multitude

Life from your ascension tearfully taught
Changing what was to accepting what is
Contained in a story lived and written
Absorbed in anguish, tearful pores
Infused in the fabric of Souls
Still trekking God's Earth abound
Faithfully walking the path you paved
Traveling alongside those who remember

Alive you are in their days and nights
A memoir, a legacy still birthing

Ruth Stallworth

When I first met Brandon in either late 2000 or early 2001, he was shopping with his mother, and my first impression was, "What a well-groomed and polite young man." He continued to come into the shop with either one or both of his parents for many years and for many gifts. When he was with his mom, it was for his expert opinion on what his dad would like, and when with his dad, it was to give the final okay on the gift selection.

While watching Brandon grow into a typical teen (the cell phone never far from his ear and I think he had started to drive), neither his behavior nor his appearance changed. Even though it was the teenage look, I never saw his undershorts or a T-shirt hanging out from under his shirt. "Yea!" for his parents.

My first question when I saw Connie and Virgil after Brandon's death was, "Where is our boy?"

You see, Brandon was one of those special young people that we all would like to claim as our own. I know that I certainly did.

Cleatrice Grisgsby

Father and Mother weep and cry
Your hearts are heavy
And I know the two of you are still wondering why
Our only son Brandon had to die

There is no answer, and there is no cure for death
But we still know how bad it hurts our hearts beneath our breast
We wake up to laughter and a simple good morning
Then before you know it, you're in mourning
For the son you loved so dear

But mother and father always remember
Brandon will always be near
In your heart, body, and soul
Because you as a mother and father
Will never ever let Brandon and his memories go

So weep as often as you like
And always remember
He's with the two of you, day and night.

Brenda Roxborough
In memory of Brandon Spight

It was a very sad day when we learned of Brandon's passing. Brian went to Brother Rice High School for grades nine through twelve, and we spent a lot of time playing sports at UDJ. He had many friends there and still at DCDS, who told him immediately about Brandon. While the boys hadn't seen each other in a while, Brian always seemed to know what all his old friends were up to, Brandon included.

As we were remembering Brandon, a funny thing Brian recalled was that he and Brandon spent plenty of time together—often cleaning tables in the DCDS lunchroom (instead of outside at recess) for *having too much fun during lunch! "Spirited boys" is what Ruth Rebold called them once.*

Sincerely,
Karen, Tim, and Brian Wing

Dear Connie,

I have never witnessed such a display of combined love, courage, and selflessness as when you read your tribute to Brandon out loud at the funeral.

This planet is very fortunate to have you and Virgil among its inhabitants, and I've always considered myself fortunate to be listed among your friends. The sheer number of guests at the funeral is testament that you are truly remarkable and extraordinary people. How else would you have produced such a remarkable and extraordinary person as Brandon?

Keith Thode

A young man we didn't even know, who attended Morehouse College, read your statement by chance and wrote me a letter.

I am not a friend of Brandon's, not a classmate but simply someone who read his obituary on the Mays Printing's website. Oftentimes I find myself reflecting on life by reading the obituaries of those who have gone on before me, and I have concluded that it is not the quantity of life, but the quality. I was truly impressed with how well he lived in seventeen years, which takes some people a lifetime to achieve.

In Brandon's obituary, there was his personal statement about his life. I was amazed at his level of awareness at such a very young age. Within his personal statement, Brandon spoke of modifying his behavior between his school community and the community in which he lived. I am not sure if Brandon was aware, but W.E.B. DuBois called that type of behavior the "double consciousness." W.E.B. DuBois expressed the notion of double consciousness as the following:

> The history of the American Negro is the history of this strife– his longing to attain self-conscious manhood, to merge his double self into a better and truer self. In this merging he wishes neither of the older selves to be lost. He does not wish to Africanize America, for America has too much to teach the world and Africa: he does not wish to bleach his Negro blood in a flood of white Americanism, for he believes that Negro blood has yet a message for the world. He simply wishes to make it possible for a man to be both a Negro and an American without being cursed and spit upon by his fellows, without losing the opportunity of self-development.

After reading Brandon's personal statement, I am convinced that he personified the notion of double consciousness.

From gathering great insight about Brandon's life through his personal statement and seeing that he was college-bound, I summed him up to be a potential candidate for Morehouse College. Although there were no schools listed that he considered attending, I felt within my heart that he was an ideal "Morehouse Man." I was tremendously impressed with his life and how he lived his life from reading his obituary that I wanted to know more. Next, I checked Facebook for additional information. There was a group for Brandon where his friends were writing stories of the good times and how much they miss him. In one person's note, they mentioned that he had been accepted into Morehouse. I was extremely happy to know that he was considering joining the ranks of outstanding young African-American *men. Ironically, I also applied to transfer into Morehouse for the fall of 2007. To know Brandon's path and mine could have very well crossed each other's is truly gratifying.*

Kody J. Melancon

FROM THE HALLS OF UNIVERSITY OF DETROIT JESUIT HIGH SCHOOL & ACADEMY

A Remembrance of Brandon by Richerd Winton

We met at U of D High in seventh grade. They had us sitting in alphabetical order, and our lockers were near each other. Brandon was an extrovert, and he loved talking to people and meeting people. He just struck up a conversation, and he loved to talk. And I was always around.

What solidified our friendship is when we played on the seventh-grade basketball team. It was a pretty good team, and we weren't the best players, so we ended up on the bench together. When we got in the game, it usually was when the team was winning. That created a bond.

When I look back, what really made us start being best friends was the school walk-a-thon, where we'd walk ten miles and people would pledge so much money per mile to raise money for the school. That involved hours of walking, and we'd be talking along the way. One defining trait for Brandon was his honesty. It was a huge thing for him, and I believe he got that from his parents. He believed he should always tell the truth. He didn't like liars, and he tried not to lie himself. During the walk-a-thon, Brandon was talking about Air Jordans, and he really had a thing for those shoes. I didn't have any Air Jordans, but I said I did. I started to feel bad about lying to him, and my conscience got the better of me. So I told him I didn't have any Jordans, that I was trying to fit in. And Brandon just stopped and looked at me. "That's probably one of the most honest things anyone has ever told me," he said. I think from that point on, he had a level of respect for me. From there, we were just best friends.

We loved going to school dances. Not having girls in our school, we'd go to dances at the Academy of the Sacred Heart or Mercy High. We'd show off our new dance moves that we practiced by watching YouTube videos. He was well-liked by the young ladies. The other guys and I waited to see which girls didn't like Brandon because maybe we'd have a shot with them.

Brandon was an assertive, confident person, and he was very intelligent. He wasn't afraid to voice his opinion on anything. When he became sick, it was the first time I saw Brandon scared or unsure. And that's when I knew something wasn't right.

One of my memories is how he loved to play sports and was just a fierce competitor, either playing basketball in someone's yard or on the golf course. Brandon really enjoyed playing golf with Mr. Spight's friends. He loved being able to say jokingly, "Some of them have played golf for longer than I've been alive, and I can beat them!" During his senior year, I caddied for him. It's hard for me now to play golf.

There are many situations now where I feel his presence and think about him. He valued honesty, loyalty, and trustworthiness. He was very reliable, and if he said he were going to help you, he'd be there for you. I try to channel that energy, that confidence and self-assuredness.

I first met you at our seventh-grade orientation. We were the only kids there with braids in our hair. I figured you had to be cool if you went to orientation with braids. Everyone knows that's a call for trouble at UDJ. And that's when our friendship started. I remember when people used to mistake us for brothers even though we swore we looked nothing alike. I think we had such a strong relationship because we shared some of the same goals and we had big dreams. You were the golf star; I was the musician. Our plan was to make it to the top of our fields and, of course, not forget about each other. Along with these dreams came some far-fetched ideas, one that included me being your caddie when you were on the pro tour, but never did they seem impossible to us, and I still believe they would have come true. Nothing seemed out of reach to you, and I'm glad I had you as a friend to instill that type of mindset in me.

Dexter Dale Dixon

We met in eighth grade. Because we sat alphabetically, with our last names we were often right next to each other. It was a lot of work turning our friendship into what it was. Our friendship has been tested time and time again, but the fact that we remained close friends until the very end proves that we passed those tests. Over the five years I knew you, I had some of the best experiences in my life.

Some of my favorites were working on school projects together, going trick-or-treating on Halloween, playing basketball and fighting over calls, going to the movies, and attending Jack-and-Jill dances. We would always have a blast no matter what we were doing. You gave me confidence and taught me to stand up for myself. Life will not be the same without you here. You knew how to make every moment worth living, even if we were just hanging out in my basement. That's something that not many people can do. I miss you, but I know you're happy and I'll meet you up there one day.

Adam Toepp

This is a bittersweet moment for me. It has been about a year now, and I still find myself from time to time wanting to call you and hang out. It has been nothing but good times with us. You were like my brother. We went to school together, hung out, and had the same group of friends. We went to the same parties, played video games all day, went to the movies, and golfed. Some of the greatest memories I have are my competition with you. If there were a more competitive person in the world, I want that person to be pointed out. We always had our rivalries whether it was golfing, grades, girls, sports of any sort, and even video games. You have always been a great competitor. You were always talented in everything you did and let the whole world know it. I would definitely say that you have inspired me to never be ashamed about anything I do and be confident in everything I do. You were one of the most down-to-earth, caring, and passionate friends I have ever had. I wish I could go back and hang out more, but we will definitely be seeing one another again one day.

R.I.P. Brandon Spight, I love you, man. You are a great friend, but more importantly you are like my brother.

Carl Roland

I would have to say my all-time favorite memory has to be when the two of us were in our senior art class. Brandon wanted to go play dodgeball in the gym, and—I hope he forgives me for snitching like this—I covered for him while he left. He told Mrs. Mooney his stomach hurt, and he went to the bathroom. After about twenty minutes went by, she was suspicious. Then Brandon shows up, shirt untucked, out of breath, and obviously sweating, and she's like, "Where did you go?" And he swears he was in the bathroom and starts holding his stomach and head. They get into an argument, and he actually gets mad that she doesn't believe him. By the time they stopped arguing, he's basically convinced her he was in the bathroom sick, and then he walks over to me grinning and says dodgeball was hype.

Chris Thomas

From his ability to take advantage of every moment of the day and have fun with it to his wisdom with the art of dance and women, Brandon was completely unique. I can honestly say that Brandon is the reason I have the slightest—and I mean very slightest—ability to dance. He told me that if I could move at all like him at dances, the girls would love me. Well, my dancing gets the girls' attention, but not at all in a good way. I never really realized it until after Brandon passed, but he showed me how much I need to try to take advantage of every day and make the most of it because we never know when it will be our time for God to bring us home.

Sean Fox

You remember when I was running for Sarge junior year? It was less than a week before elections, and I was starting to lose my cool. The pressure was getting to me big time, and it was showing. I was snapping at kids that I normally was cordial to, short-tempered with an unnecessarily huge ego. Basically, I was being everything short of the leadership position I was running for. You were the only one to actually pull me aside and ask me if things were getting too heavy for me. On top of that, you were the only one who reminded me how important it was to keep my head when everyone around me just wanted to watch me explode. And even later in the day, when I was about three seconds away from punching out a freshman just because he said he wasn't voting for me, you were the only one whispering reminders of fortitude behind me. I don't think you realized the impact you had on me during that time. Or maybe you did. In regards to that election, it wouldn't have mattered to me if I had lost (even though I know you secretly wanted to take credit for the victory). Knowing that you had my back was a victory in itself. But that's you, naturally defending people and helping them out. Take care, Brandon. We are all better people because of you.

Tony Maccio

I want to start this letter by telling you both that I love and thank you for all you did for me since the seventh grade. It was an honor for you to embrace me as one of your own children. I think if it weren't for you two and Brandon, I don't think I would have made it this far. From the bottom of my heart, I love you two like my own parents. I will make you proud of me.

Devin Mack

It has been a year since this world lost him, and not one day goes by that I don't think the world is worse off because of that. Your son was a man who brought light to every moment of every day for so many people, including me. His smile alone sent an echo of hope, joy, and the grandeur of life. I believe Brandon was one of the greatest gifts God gave our world, our U of D community, and you.

So many people were touched by your son. Today, I sit here and think to myself, and I am jealous that Brandon is not here. I'm jealous because he can't shake my hand and give me some confidence during the day or crack a smile that would light up a room. I'm jealous because I miss him and his presence, along with his values, his love for life, his humor and smile, his leadership, and his strength in all situations.

I know that Brandon's life still inspires and gives hope to so many. The most powerful thing is that it still does. Brandon affected me so much during his amazing and wonderful life that every single moment during my day, I can feel him helping, guiding, and showing everyone what is best. And it's not his memory. It's him. He lives today in every smile I see. He lives in every selfless act, every laugh, and every heartbeat. He lives in the best in me and everyone who graduated from UDJ last year. He lives in passion, he lives in leadership, he lives in love, and he lives by touching every single person who ever met him.

Tim Deters

Brandon, I never had the opportunity to meet you. We may have passed in the UDJ halls from time to time, but never did I have the privilege of knowing you. It has been some time now since you were last here with us. It has been difficult for some and even harder for others. However, your death has brought us all together. I joined your Facebook group a couple months ago. I spent some time reading all the memories about you, from your classmates to siblings. It was touching. I learned more and more about you as I continued reading. I really wish I did not have to come to know you this way. This year I had the opportunity of being the golf team manager. The team was quite successful this season. Many of my close friends are golfers, and from them I have been able to come to find out who you really were. From the golf trips in the summer to playing on the course, you really were a remarkable guy. The golf team won the Central Division and placed tenth in state finals. We did this for you. We knew how much you loved golf. Also an award was created in your name. It was given to the golfer who best exemplifies the qualities you had: leadership, charisma, sportsmanship, and dedication. We want your legacy to live on. One way for the future U of D Cubs to know who you were is through this award. Hopefully guys will strive to be like you. Every day I wear my Brandon L. Spight bracelet to live up to who you were. I know I cannot be you. But I can at least try.

Matt Ippel

I got to have regular interactions with Brandon from our freshman French class with Madame Barteld. During this class, I developed a friendship with Brandon. I would have many more classes with Brandon and great experiences in and out of school. Brandon was a kid just like the rest of us, known to always have a word for any faculty member who was unfair to him and to savage your books and belongings or flip your backpack at school. He and Richerd Winton were actually the first people to savage me one day in the cafeteria. However, Brandon never let his teenage ambitions and pranks hurt someone. This came from morals and ethics that Brandon held, which led him to express care for fellow students and human beings. I remember him saying sometimes, "That's just not right," or he told me once while watched Hotel Rwanda, "That's not savage; that's just ruthless."

However, the one thing that was core to Brandon's nature and behavior was that he never accepted what he was told without analyzing it first, and he would never lay down and let anyone disregard his rights as a person and a student without speaking up. When we would have debates ranging from music to politics to religion, he caused me to question quite often what I thought to be true. If after analyzing my belief/premise properly, I no longer believed it to be true, then it wasn't worth believing in the first place.

One example was our trigonometry class with Mrs. Coury. We clowned a bit too much, and Brandon was often a key ringleader of the clowning and mischief. It even got to the point where Mrs. Coury put him in the front row, despite his protest and argument that she was making him the scapegoat of classroom rowdiness. He would be vindicated as classroom noise continued and even intensified, which Brandon was never slow to point out. Mrs Coury was never told in the beginning of the year that Brandon rarely lost an argument.

Medvis Jackson

Charles Bryson:
My bro, my bro
My bro, my bro
Tears will never show
Memories just won't go
Wasn't expecting this blow
Not forgotten but you missed
How is the past time in bliss?
Well, not too much, you see this

No need to go into further detail
Golfers at the high try to follow your trail
Yeah, I know many things have changed
I thought it was you when my phone ranged
We weren't close for too long long
Something like a couple of years
Long enough to develop a bond
It hurts to know that you're gone
I know you here, but you know what I mean
I smiled when I heard your song
"Work on the kitchen table"
We listen to going toward Maple
"Work, work"
Chanted in your Escort
Excuse me, "The Board"
Walking this journey of life
I feel you as one of my escorts
Did you have to ask to be one of mine?
We'll toast in one of heaven's courts
One day ... one day
Lol, naw this Sunday, you silly B
From a stranger to a brother
A brother from another
My, my bro
Tears will never show
How much you've missed
Come on, you know I don't cry
From Charles Bryson "Chay B" to B. Spight
Love you Brandon ... 5 stars

EPILOGUE

Brandon, you lived the UDJ motto of "A Man for Others." You exemplified at a young age the power of the human spirit and the ability and capacity to connect with others, young and old. You made a positive difference in so many lives. And like you, we each have the power within us to make a positive difference in the lives of others.

We each will likely face a life-altering event at some point in our lives. Focusing on the needs of others can give us strength and allow us to find new pathways forward.

When we lose those we love, we are impacted profoundly and inexplicably. Accurately describing that loss is impossible to put into words or explain to others in any kind of rational or coherent manner. Loss binds us to the past with memories and stories because of the familiar comfort we seek.

We expect to outlive our parents. Intellectually, we try to understand that we may outlive a spouse, a significant other, a family member, or a friend. But we don't expect to outlive our children. A child holds and embodies our future. A child is our legacy for what comes next for generations to come. A child embodies our hopes, our dreams. The loss of a child alters our everyday lives and shatters our framework and image of the future. We're left in a dark abyss without walls, floor, or ceiling, nothing to grab or hold on to. Rather we just fall deeper and deeper, unable to see any light to the future.

We fight to find the strength to get through just one single moment, one hour, one day at a time. We lean on our spiritual beliefs, friends, family, and others to help carry us along on our grief journey. We strive to gradually come to a place of deep empathy for others and realize that we can each make a positive difference in the lives of others. We begin to channel our deep grief into powerful and life-changing work for the benefit of others.

This book is not intended to tell anyone how to deal with unimaginable loss, personal tragedy, or adversity. This is a story about a young man who exemplified the importance of connecting with others, the love of family, and the positive impact individual actions can have on others. Brandon is an example of the great capacity we each have within us to give, care about, and support others. The resilience of the human spirit, even during our most tragic times, lives on.

This book is a story of sacrifice and giving. Even during our greatest moments of despair, we still have the capacity to make a difference. Organ donation, the ultimate gift of life, can make a remarkable difference in the lives of others.

ACKNOWLEDGEMENTS

Writing this book was not my idea. I admit this may seem odd and emotionally detached, especially to those of you who are acutely aware of my relationship with my son. Brandon and I had a closeness that I didn't know could exist between a mom and her son. So not having a desire to write a book about Brandon had nothing to do with the uniqueness of our bond. Rather my overpowering, debilitating grief literally took control of any rational thought that would have led me in that direction. It wasn't until it was suggested by not one but two unsuspecting individuals that I began to consider the possibility. I abruptly dismissed the first suggestion.

However, when another person mentioned a book about Brandon, an eerie feeling came over me. Was this idea actually coming from a higher power? Was it Brandon emphatically saying, "Mom, a book about me! Of course you gotta do this!"

So my heartfelt thanks must go first to Glenda Vicks, who through persistent phone calls to me insisted that a book be written because her dreams would not cease until I committed to this project. Additionally Karen Dumas took a personal interest in creating a legacy for a boy whom she had never met. I will forever be thankful to both of you for enlightening a grieving mom to possibilities beyond her realm.

I owe tremendous gratitude to my sisters in my heart—Cheryl Gambrell Harris, Margaret Alston, Carol Stoll, Chie Handy,

Adrienne Smith, Lisa Stout, Vicki Watson, and Gwen Arrington—for providing the unselfish support that even I didn't know I needed. Cheryl, you connected with me daily and later spent countless hours with me editing the book for accuracy. Margaret, you offered your unexpected visits that always included your good-for-the-soul meals. Carol, you gave me your wisdom and was the best co-mom Brandon could have. Chie, you offered your religious advice and amazing spiritual words that symbolically associated Brandon with Jesus Christ. Adrienne, thanks for your sympathetic and nonjudgmental understanding of a grieving mom's untimely and unreasonable requests. Lisa, you provided your compassionate words and spent time with me at grief counseling meetings. Vicki, you offered your intuitiveness and joined me in what became cleansing sessions. Gwen, thanks for being a devoted friend, notwithstanding that we are connected by blood. But most of all, I am immensely grateful that none of you will ever forget Brandon and the ways he impacted your life.

Thank you to my girls—Brie Cocroft, Melita Alston Smith, Kezia McAllister, Jillian Coleman, Erica Alexander, Whitney Brown, and Kyra Bolden—whose purpose in my life I now clearly understand, for each one of you provided infallible devotion that any mom would cherish from a daughter.

Thank you to Brandon's siblings, Diane, Virgil Jr., Harlan, and Darnell, who offered a level of sibling camaraderie that Brandon loved and appreciated.

I would be remiss if I didn't mention the entire University of Detroit Jesuit High School and Academy (UDJ) community. Forgive me for not personally naming more of you, but I must give Father Karl Kiser, Principal Susan Rowe, and development officers Mary Barden and Thomas O'Keefe considerable praise for how they demonstrated such immense compassion for us during this unspeakable tragedy during their tenure at the High.

To Coach Paul Diehl, the young men on the golf team, and

all the other UDJ young men whose hearts were obviously broken by Brandon's death, we appreciate the strength you provided to our family.

To Pastor and Mrs. Ronald Griffin, thanks for your pastoral guidance and committed relationship to our family.

To all who wrote letters, poems, and remembrances about Brandon, without them this book would be incomplete. Please know that your words are treasured.

Many, many thanks to Patricia Montemurri, who took on the arduous task of helping me complete this project. Because of numerous delays and derailments, it would not have come to fruition without your help.

To the Board of Directors of the Brandon Lee Spight Memorial Foundation—Carl Stoll, Cheryl Gambrell Harris, Tommy Alston, Cleophus Boyd, Jillian Coleman, Melita Alston Smith, and Doreen Odom—we appreciate how you voluntarily provided a wide, well-informed range of diverse opinions and advice.

Thank you to the Gift of Life staff: Remonia Chapman, Sheila Alston, Crystal Peeples, Josh Angel, Cindy Kirschbaum, and Penny Colhurst. Only special people do what you do.

Thank you to Amy Wolterstorff. Through your wisdom, you encouraged the emotional wording I was reluctant to share.

Thank you to Margaret Alston, Karen Schrock, and Adrienne Smith for proofreading and editing. I appreciate your meaningful opinions, thoughts and ideas.

Last, but certainly not least, I owe my life to my husband, Virgil Spight, who even in his own agony refused to allow me to perish.

MORE ABOUT ORGAN DONATION

Most organ donations come from people who have passed on. But organ donations also come from living donors. In 2017, about four out of five organ donations came from deceased donors. The generosity from one deceased donor can save the lives of eight people and enhance the lives of over seventy-five people with tissue donation. Living donors, who may donate a kidney or part of their liver, for example, comprise about 20 percent of organ donations.

If you want to be considered for organ donation in the event of your passing, please register with the Michigan Organ Donor Registry through the Michigan Secretary of State, www.michigan. gov/sos. Your Michigan driver's license or Michigan ID card will be printed with a heart logo to indicate that you've signed up. Please let your family members know of your wishes also.

To learn more about organ donation, please visit www.organdonor. gov or www.giftoflifemichigan.org. No age limit prevents one from signing up on the Michigan Organ Donor Registry. There is no charge to you or your family for donation.

Most major religions support organ and tissue donation. Chronic diseases such as diabetes, high blood pressure, and even some cancers do not necessarily preclude you from donating organs or tissue. Donating organs is a surgical procedure that should not affect customary funeral arrangements or alter body appearance.

Make sure your next-of-kin, guardian, or friends are aware of your decision about organ donation. Signing up on the Michigan Organ Donor Registry ensures that your wish to be an organ and tissue donor will be fulfilled.

Questions

Contact Remonia Chapman, Program Director for Minority Organ Transplant Tissue Education Program, 3861 Research Park Drive, Ann Arbor MI 48108, rchapman@golm.org.

BRANDON LEE SPIGHT MEMORIAL FOUNDATION

The Brandon Lee Spight Memorial Foundation is a nonprofit operating within the 501(c)(3) guidelines.

The mission of the Brandon Lee Spight Memorial Foundation (BLSMF): To receive and administer funds to youth from diverse cultures and lower economic backgrounds which will provide them an opportunity for self empowerment through education.

The vision of the Brandon Lee Spight Memorial Foundation (BLSMF): We are providing an educational opportunity to youth from diverse cultures and lower economic backgrounds who perpetuate the legacy of Brandon Lee Spight by demonstrating character, integrity, promise, commitment and dedication to excellence in academics, athletics, and personal behavior. The BLSMF recognizes and supports such youth through various avenues of resources and assistance to enable them to realize their potential for self empowerment as established by Brandon Spight.

Brandon Lee Spight Memorial Foundation (BLSMF)
P.O. Box 21-432
Detroit, MI 48221
Planbspight.org
blsplanb@gmail.com